MW00561889

LEARNING
in a
BURNING
HOUSE

*Educational Inequality, Ideology,
and (Dis)Integration*

LEARNING
in a
BURNING
HOUSE

Educational Inequality, Ideology, and (Dis)Integration

Sonya Douglass Horsford
Foreword by Marian Wright Edelman

Teachers College, Columbia University
New York and London

Published by Teachers College Press, 1234 Amsterdam Avenue, New York, NY 10027

Chapters 1, 2, and 4 are adapted and expanded from the following sources: "Mixed Feelings about Mixed Schools: Superintendents on the Complex Legacy of School Desegregation" by S. D. Horsford, 2010, *Educational Administration Quarterly, 46*(3), 287–321. Copyright 2010 by *Educational Administration Quarterly.* Reprinted by permission of SAGE Publications. "Vestiges of Desegregation: Superintendent Perspectives on Educational Inequality and (Dis)Integration in the Post-Civil Rights Era" by S. D. Horsford, 2011, *Urban Education 46*(1), 34–54. Copyright 2011 by Urban Education. Reprinted by permission of SAGE Publications.

Chapter 2 is adapted and expanded from the following sources: "From *Negro* Student to *Black* Superintendent: Counternarratives on Segregation and Desegregation" by S. D. Horsford, 2009, *The Journal of Negro Education, 78*(2), 172–187. Copyright 2009 by *The Journal of Negro Education.* With kind permission from Springer + Business Media: "Black Superintendents on Educating Black Students in Separate and Unequal Contexts" by S. D. Horsford, 2010, *The Urban Review, 42*(1), 58–79. Copyright 2010 by *The Urban Review.*

Library of Congress Cataloging-in-Publication Data

Horsford, Sonya Douglass.
    Learning in a burning house : educational inequality, ideology, and (dis)integration / Sonya Douglass Horsford ; foreword by Marian Wright Edelman.
      p. cm.
    Includes bibliographical references and index.
    ISBN 978-0-8077-5176-3 (pbk.)—ISBN 978-0-8077-5177-0 (hardcover)
    1. African American schools—History. 2. African American school superintendents—History. 3. School integration—United States—History. 4. Racism in education—United States—History. 5. Discrimination in education—United States—History. I. Title.
    LC2741.H67 2011
    448.2'421—dc22

                                         2010045278

ISBN 978-0-8077-5176-3 (paperback)
ISBN 978-0-8077-5177-0 (hardcover)

Printed on acid-free paper
Manufactured in the United States of America

18 17 16 15 14 13 12 11   8 7 6 5 4 3 2 1

To Kil Cha and Gilbert Douglass—
For the sacrifices you made.

To Benjamin, Bryson, and Ella—
For teaching me life's greatest lessons.

And to the "firefighters" who have accepted the call to serve children
selflessly, tirelessly, and fairly.

This is for you.

We have fought long and hard for integration, as I believe we should have, and I know that we will win. But I've come to believe we're integrating into a burning house.

—Dr. Martin Luther King, Jr.

Contents

Foreword

In *Learning in a Burning House,* Sonya Douglass Horsford examines the ways in which our nation is still falling short in providing equal chances for quality education to Black children. Statistics show racial resegregation in our public schools has been rising slowly and systematically over the last 2 decades, confirming the sad truth that the dream Dr. Martin Luther King considered one of the greatest victories of the Civil Rights Movement—the ending of separate and unequal schools and the desegregation of our nation's schools—is unraveling before our eyes without having fully lived up to its promise.

African Americans have always seen education as a key to life and freedom. In his autobiography *Narrative of the Life of Frederick Douglass,* our great abolitionist leader taught us that to educate a person is to "forever unfit him to be a slave," but to deny a person education is to "[shut him] up in mental darkness." I remember growing up in the 1940s and 1950s South—an inquisitive young girl barred from the library, the pool, and other public facilities because of my race. Our unequally funded Black school's library had hand-me-down, out-of-date books from White schools. The external world put a lot of obstacles in my way and told me that Black children weren't as valuable as White children, but I didn't believe it because my parents and teachers said it wasn't so. My parents valued education and reading and made sure we always had books in our home, even when we did not have a second pair of shoes. At school, our teachers did not allow us to fail. They knew their mission was to prepare us for the future. And there was a strong belief in our community that education was a way out that could give us the means to change the world.

But today millions of children who need hope and a way out receive neither of these things, and too many adults tolerate this. Legal segregation has ended, but inequality is alive and well and segregation is still occurring all over America. Without a good education, millions of America's 14 million poor children (this is before the recession's numbers) will remain poor throughout their lives and many will become trapped in the Cradle to Prison Pipeline® crisis that leads to dropping out of school, arrest, and incarceration at earlier and earlier ages. As President Obama has said, education is still the strongest weapon against social inequality and the best path to opportunity in America. But inequities in educational funding, resources, and opportunities have placed so many poor and minority children in low-performing schools with inadequate facilities and ineffective teachers.

Practices such as tracking, social promotion, and out-of-school suspensions and expulsions resulting from one-size-fits-all zero tolerance policies contribute to the discouragement and disengagement experienced by many poor children and children of color. So instead of being the great equalizer, American education has perpetuated and increased inequality, with the result that poor children stay poor, poorly educated, and unskilled. Rather than providing a way out of poverty and discrimination, American schools too often mimic the economic and racial disparities that poison the rest of American society, with devastating results for children and our nation. It is a national catastrophe that over 80% of Black children cannot read or compute at grade level in fourth, eighth, or twelfth grade—if they have not already dropped out. And it is indefensible that a Black boy born in 2001 has a one in three chance of going to prison in his lifetime.

As sociologist Ray Rist put it powerfully 40 years ago, "if one desires this society to retain its present social class configuration and the disproportional access to wealth, power, social and economic mobility, medical care, and the choice of life styles, *one should not disturb the methods of education [operating in America]*" (emphasis added).

Is this what we really desire for our nation's and children's future? Or are we prepared to stand up, speak out, raise a ruckus, and insist our schools—all of them, from traditional public schools and public charters to magnet and community schools—live up to the promise of educating every child and replacing the prison pipeline with a pipeline to college, career, and productive work?

I hope Dr. Horsford's book will spur much discussion about the greatest national security threat faced by our nation: millions of illiterate and poorly prepared children unprepared to meet the future demands in an increasingly competitive globalizing economy. Wake up, America!

—*Marian Wright Edelman*

REFERENCES

Children's Defense Fund. (2007). America's cradle to prison pipeline: A Children's Defense Fund Report. Retrieved August 12, 2010, from http://www.childrensdefense.org/child-research-data-publications/data/cradle-prison-pipeline-report-2007-full-highres.pdf

Douglass, F. (1963). *Narrative of the life of Frederick Douglass, an American slave*. Garden City, NY: Doubleday. (Original work published 1845)

Rist, R. (1970). Student social class and teacher expectations: The self-fulfilling prophecy in ghetto education. *Harvard Educational Review, 40*(3), 411–451.

Acknowledgments

I am grateful for the experiences that have fueled my curiosity about separate and unequal education and the people who helped me develop my views in ways that made this book possible.

First, I would not have completed this project without the encouragement and guidance of caring and demanding mentors both in and beyond academia, including Linda Tillman, M. Christopher Brown II, and my dear friend, Diane Hughes Pollard, all of whom, according to their own brand of inquiry, consistently asked, "Is it finished yet?"

My thanks to my intellectual colleagues at the University of Nevada, Las Vegas and those at other institutions, including Jeff Brooks, Judy Alston, Enrique Alemán, Kathryn Bell McKenzie, Sylvia Lazos, George Theoharis, Camille Wilson Cooper, Gaetane Jean-Marie, Mark Gooden, Elizabeth Murakami-Ramalho, Tambra Jackson, Adrienne Dixson, Terah Venzant-Chambers, T. Elon Dancy II, and James Earl Davis. Thank you to the anonymous reviewers at Teachers College Press, and to Meg Hartmann, Lori Tate, and especially Brian Ellerbeck for seeing the potential in my "book-to-be" and ensuring its "care and feeding" along the way.

Special thanks to my sister scholars and "first ladies" of educational leadership—Patrice McClellan, April Peters, Karen Beard, Latish Reed, Lisa Bass, and Cosette Grant-Overton. You have sustained me with your intellect, compassion, conversation, and strength of spirit. And to my students at UNLV and those who I have had the pleasure of meeting through the Holmes Scholars™ Program and UCEA Jackson Scholars Program, you have been a great source of inspiration. Stay true to your work and to yourselves.

I want to thank Marian Wright Edelman for penning the foreword to this book and for her steadfast leadership as an advocate for children everywhere. Many thanks also to Lisa Clayton Robinson, Jeanne Middleton-Hairston, Rebekah Piper, and the entire Children's Defense Fund Freedom Schools® family for "becoming firefighters" for fair and just education. Harambee!

I must thank my best friend and partner, Steven, for his critical eye and encouraging words, along with my sister, Sandra, and my brother, Don, for their continued love, kindness, and support. I am not particularly pleasant to be around when a deadline is looming, but they endured, and I am grateful. I also want to thank Pamela Horsford, Angela Williams, Brooke Reid, Brittani Reid, Booker Reid, and those family members who had the fortune of enduring this process from afar, including my dear grandmother Candis Douglas, the loving matriarch of our family. I am eternally grateful for my parents, Kil Cha and Gilbert Douglass, Jr., my sons, Benjamin and Bryson, and my daughter, Ella, to whom this book is dedicated.

Finally, I owe a special debt of gratitude to the former school superintendents who took the time to share their personal reflections and perspectives on school segregation, desegregation, and the future of U.S. education. Your professional insight and wisdom has expanded our knowledge of educational inequality, ideology, and integration in important ways. Thank you for leading the way.

Introduction

"Desegregation is a joke."

I could hardly believe my eyes. In my quest for interesting historical perspectives and remarks about desegregation, I stumbled across these four words quoted from the late singer and songwriter Nina Simone. The undersized sentence held oversized meaning, and I immediately became intrigued yet saddened by its resonance. Simone's words, much like her melancholy lyrics and brooding voice, captured the disappointment and pain you feel when you've been lied to; the hardness that develops when you have decided you can trust no more. It was almost worse than Langston Hughes's oft-quoted stench and sagging of a dream deferred because it suggested that the dream, in this case desegregation, was never serious to begin with.

It was this sentiment of disappointment and cynicism expressed by African Americans who lived under segregation, questioned, and in many cases regretted desegregation, that grabbed me several years ago. How could this be? Some blamed desegregation for destroying the tight-knit, supportive, and self-contained Black communities that supported Black children and families. Others said it created many of the problems of underachievement, high special education placements, behavioral referrals, and high school dropout rates that plague Black education today. Others engaged in what Lani Guinier (2004) described as the "eerie nostalgia" of the golden era of segregation for Black people, reveling in memories of communal Black villages that were home to Black barbers, doctors, markets, preachers, businesses, watchful neighbors, nurturing teachers, *good* schools, and a sense of community.

THE DESEGREGATION DILEMMA

Michele Foster (1997) documented these feelings and experiences through the oral and life histories of three generations of educators in *Black Teach-*

ers on Teaching. Mwalimu J. Shujaa (1996) examined the political and racialized contexts of desegregation policies in his volume *Beyond Deseg-regation: The Politics of Quality in African American Schooling.* In 2004, both Charles Ogletree's *All Deliberate Speed: Reflections on the First Half-Century of Brown v. Board of Education* and Derrick Bell's *Silent Covenants: Brown v. Board of Education and the Unfulfilled Hopes for Racial Reform* extended the discussion of Black education before and after desegregation through the authors' unique perspectives as Civil Rights attorneys during the 1960s and 1970s in (notably different) ways that shaped politics, the law, and American race relations then and now. Bell went so far as to say that the *Brown* decision was nothing more than a "magnificent mirage" that was "dulled by resistance" and "more symbolic than real." He was not alone in this assessment. In fact, in 1980, while dean of the University of Oregon Law School, Bell offered, in his edited volume *Shades of Brown*, an impor-tant collection of writings by legal and education scholars who 25 years after *Brown*, "expressed perspectives on the school desegregation cam-paign that depart[ed] from the unwritten Civil Rights Commandment: Thou shalt not publicly criticize" and broke "the public value of silence that so many have used as balm for their growing concerns" (p. ix) about the ineffectiveness of school desegregation.

I was captivated. Curious. Confused. For all these years I thought de-segregation was a good thing. A great thing for Black people. Segregation was wrong, so desegregation must be right. If it wasn't, why would we celebrate and commemorate the anniversary of the *Brown v. Board of Edu-cation* decision of 1954 every May? Thurgood Marshall and the NAACP fought for it. Drs. Kenneth and Mamie Clark testified against it. Martin Luther King, Jr., died for it, and his wife Coretta Scott asserted, "Segrega-tion was wrong when it was forced by White people, and I believe it is still wrong when it is requested by Black people."

How could anyone critique the movement for Black progress through integration and inclusion? The resolve, suffering, and sacrifice made by Black people who wanted Black children to have the same educational access, resources, opportunities, and subsequent rewards and quality of life associated with educational attainment as White children? There had to be something special about their insight and their take on the issue. After all, they were raised in it. They lived and worked through it. This generation of Black folks had more firsthand knowledge and perspec-tive than my generation (Generation X) and the non-Black scholars who never attended all-Black segregated schools could ever have, combined.

But perhaps, as Gary Orfield (2005) suggested, these individuals were peering through "rose-colored glasses" as they recalled their lives under segregation, compelling them to long for the beauty of an era that never truly existed the way they say it did. Or the ways in which Faustine Jones (1981) documented in *The Traditional Model of Excellence: Dunbar High School in Little Rock, Arkansas,* or Vanessa Siddle Walker (1996) reported in her historical ethnography, *Their Highest Potential: An African American School Community in the Segregated South,* which described the valued qualities of Caswell County Training Center.

In his 2008 review of research on segregated and contemporary Black schooling in *Teachers College Record,* Jerome Morris argued that the growing counternarrative of valued segregated schools and limitations of *Brown* should inform how education researchers and policymakers framed urban education and school reform efforts.

> Whereas there is a national preoccupation with standardized measures of student outcomes, it is equally important to consider how the relationships among individuals and institutions (e.g., schools, communities, educators, families, and children) can also lead to effective schooling. (p. 727)

Similarly, the preoccupation with the number of minority students in majority-minority schools as compared with their majority counterparts in minority or majority schools misses the point. Although it may advance *desegregation,* it does not get us to what Adair (1984) described as the "more credible goal" of *integration.*

DESEGREGATION V. INTEGRATION

In 2006, I was lucky enough to meet and have a brief conversation with the late Asa Hilliard. It was a chance encounter in the hallways at the annual meeting of the American Educational Research Association in San Francisco, and just 2 weeks earlier I had successfully defended my dissertation prospectus, which sparked my growing interest in the dilemmas of educational ideology and inequality. I was nervously but excitedly describing to him the aim of my research and outlined my plan to interview retired Black school superintendents who attended segregated schools to get their perspectives on school integration. To which he replied, "Integration never happened."

After my heart started beating again and my mind wondered why this chance encounter could not have happened 2 years earlier, Dr. Hilliard immediately put me at ease. With his knowing eyes and smile, he explained to me the very important distinction between integration and desegregation and how, in his opinion, integration never really happened in any meaningful way because students were still segregated by race in their "desegregated" schools. Based on this conversation, I searched high and low for operational definitions that captured Dr. Hilliard's comments and those of the countless Black scholars and educators who continue to emphasize this very important difference.

While many people continue to use the terms interchangeably, Adair (1984) aptly explained the distinct meanings of desegregation and integration in his very important book, *Desegregation: The Illusion of Black Progress*. In it, he defined *desegregation* as the "physical reassignment of children and staff to change the existing racial composition in schools," as compared with *integration*, defined by the U.S. Commission on Civil Rights as "a quality of education and interpersonal interaction based on the positive acceptance of individual and group differences as well as similarities" (p. 168). Ogletree (2004), however, described integration as "a means of achieving a goal, not the goal itself," which he declares is "creating a new community founded on a new form of respect and tolerance" (p. 301). His definition echoes the one provided by Dr. Martin Luther King, Jr., in his speech, "The Ethical Demands for Integration," in which he characterized integration as "creative . . . more profound and far reaching than desegregation," "genuine intergroup, interpersonal doing," and "the ultimate goal of our national community" (1962/1986, p. 118).

Despite the significance of the distinction between desegregation as a short-term goal and means to the ultimate goal of integration (Adair, 1984; Bell, 1976, 1980; King, 1962/1986; Ogletree, 2004, Walters 2008), contemporary advocates for school integration continue to focus on the role of interracial contact in reducing individual prejudice and discrimination. In their 2008 book, *Both Sides Now*, Wells and colleagues do a better job of focusing on these aspects of "interpersonal action" and "positive acceptance," which too often have taken a backseat to data that document the degrees of "body mixing" in schools, communities, and various regions of the country. While the interpersonal benefits of desegregation are present in the literature on and policies supporting multicultural education, diversity, and inclusion, they often become trumped by an emphasis on the numbers of minority students who attend majority-minority schools as compared with their majority counterparts. In an effort to demonstrate the benefits of interpersonal action and positive acceptance, Wells and her colleagues present the favorable experiences of desegregation through case studies of students who attended mixed schools.

This research, however, and other studies like it, do not address the lack of "full participation by minorities at all levels of the educational system" resulting from the "one-way street" of desegregation policies and practices (Adair, 1984, p. 168). This continues to be the case as reported by the National Center for Education Statistics (2006), which found that during the 2003–04 school year, more than 83.1% of teachers were White, 7.9% were Black, only 6.2% were Hispanic, and 75% of the total number of teachers were women. Similarly, 82.4% of school principals were White, while 10.6% were Black (largely in central cities and charter schools), and only 5.3% were Hispanic. Additional research shows that the demographic profile of individuals attending college to become schoolteachers and administrators is strikingly similar. How does this inadequate representation of people of color in the educational system and along the pipeline of future educators and policymakers impact the effectiveness of school desegregation efforts, and thus, the goals of improved student learning, educational quality, and academic achievement?

In their 2005 book, Boger and Orfield ask, "Must the South turn back?" But scholars who hearken to voices of color and the experiential knowledge they bring, are questioning the qualitative value of how much the South or any other region has really moved forward in the first place (Adair, 1984; Bell, 2004; Guinier, 2004; Horsford, 2008, 2009b, 2010b; Morris, 2008, 2009; Walker, 2000). These researchers are working to gain insight from the individuals who suffered at the hands of the empty promise of integration and are able to provide informed perspectives that discern the depths and influence of institutional racism in education. Such educators and policymakers who value the standpoint and perspectives of the people, families, and communities that have been doubly aggrieved by the "illusion of Black progress" are no longer willing to continue to nurture the mythical trope of school integration from which we allegedly are turning back. It is time to address what sociologist, and expert witness in *Brown*, Dr. Kenneth B. Clark (1995) observed 40 years after the landmark decision and subsequent efforts to desegregate schools. With the advantage of hindsight, he noted, "It is difficult to understand that these attempts, busing, affirmative action, or devices, or words, or approaches, are used to disguise the continuation of American racism."

CENTERING RACE AND VOICE IN THE DESEGREGATION DISCOURSE

Although *Brown* and school desegregation remains a popular topic in education research, it is often to the dismay of education scholars and practitioners who do not see any present-day relevance to this issue of "the past." That was then, this is now. The laws have changed and it is time to address the contemporary educational issues of today. The inherent role of race and racism in desegregation research and policy invokes various feelings and opinions among various people, often along racial, geographic, and generational lines. Despite the central function that race and its subsequent meaning plays in the conceptualization and implementation of desegregation policies and strategies, and the resistance that often follows, race fails to be contextualized in any meaningful way in the mainstream desegregation discourse. It is included as a variable, but not analyzed as a construct that has overwhelming implications for why we are witnessing record-breaking rates of resegregation, why the "credible goal" of integration eluded us, and why the laws and practice of segregation were ever established and sanctioned in the first place.

But what is even more troubling is the extremely contradictory ways research on desegregation is conceptualized, conducted, analyzed, interpreted, and reported, depending on one's ideological perspective and racial standpoint. Not that these differences are not to be welcomed or expected as we work together to identify ways to improve education in ways essential to a thriving democracy. Obviously, in the cause for racially and socially just education, there are Black people who continue to support desegregation for educational equality and White people who question its effectiveness in achieving that equality. There is, however, a striking difference in how race influences one's optimism or cynicism for desegregation strategies. The glaring disconnect between those who recall the *Brown* decision with great nostalgia, and others who point to its failure as evidenced by the present state of Black education, often is informed by racial identity and standpoint, or what Walters (2008) observed as "the differing perspectives on racial problems that are shaped by the race and class position of the viewer" (p. 15). Quite naturally, he concluded, "this distance between viewpoints leads to different judgments about the quality of fairness or justice belonging to an event or practice" (p. 15).

In her 2004 article in the *Journal of American History*, Guinier presented a legal argument concerning the limits of the *Brown* decision, which I believe has clear implications for the future of education. In the context of *Brown* and racial desegregation, she presented *racial liberalism* as an ideological framework that "emphasized the corrosive effect of individual prejudice and the importance of interracial contact in promoting tolerance" and the "damaging effects of segregation on black personality development to secure legal victory as well as white middle-class sympathy" (p. 95). She further argued that the problem of "interest-divergence" or the coalitions that were established among liberal White northerners and conservative southern Whites resulted in *desegregation* rather than *integration*. Racial liberalism's focus on the ideals of colorblindness (color or race doesn't matter), meritocracy (access and achievement are based on individual worthiness), and neutrality of the law (all persons are treated equally under the law) was based on a definition of equality as "the absence of formal, legal barriers that separated the races" rather than "a fair and just distribution of resources" (p. 95). These important distinctions between and among our definitions of *equality, justice, desegregation, integration,* and *opportunity* are where the debate that informs education policy lies.

Rooted in legal studies, critical race theory (CRT) places race and racism at the center of a problem or inquiry, simultaneously challenging the ideals of colorblindness, meritocracy, incrementalism, and neutrality of the law. It puts these concepts up against the principles of interest convergence, interest divergence, Whiteness as property, and the permanence of racism, and uses the experiences, stories, knowledge, and perspectives of people and communities of color as a basis of understanding and ultimately a tool for positive social change. As a theoretical framework, CRT provides a lens through which a meaningful analysis of desegregation policy and its effectiveness in moving our nation's schools toward positive integrated schooling experiences is, indeed, critical. Not only does it interrogate the historical and pervasive relationships among race, class, geography, property, and power in U.S. education and society; it also paves the way for activist scholarship and education praxis that seek to dismantle racialized hierarchies and uses of power, as Angela Davis would say, by "grasping things at the root."

Another important feature of CRT is the voice-of-color thesis, which suggests that based on historical experiences of oppression and encounters with discrimination, people of color bear a "presumed competence" to discuss matters of race and racism (Delgado & Stefancic, 2000). It also recognizes the possibilities of adding richness to a discourse that has failed to hearken student and educator voices of color on matters concerning race in education (Alemán, 2007; DeCuir & Dixson, 2004; Dixson & Rousseau, 2005; Horsford, 2009, 2010a, 2010b; Ladson-Billings, 2005; Ladson-Billings & Tate, 1995; López, 2003; Lopez & Parker, 2003; Parker, Deyhle, & Villenas, 1999; Parker & Lynn, 2002; Parker & Villalpondo, 2007; Solórzano & Yosso, 2002). Throughout this book, I present the perspectives of former Black school superintendents who attended segregated schools as students, and led desegregated school districts as administrators, to offer an informed view that all too often is forgotten in education research. As Murtadha and Watts (2005) observed:

> The omission of Black leadership narratives . . . limits our ability to develop ways to improve schools and communities for children who live in poverty and children of color who are becoming the majority of the nation's schools. (p. 591)

BLACK SUPERINTENDENT PERSPECTIVES

In my attempt to gain personal and professional insight from educational leaders who actually had attended all-Black segregated schools and, as

superintendents, were responsible for leading, improving, and representing desegregated school districts and systems, I had the good fortune of
spending time with eight former superintendents in eight one-on-one interviews in various parts of the United States. Through network sampling,
I identified and selected eight participants who satisfied three criteria: (1)
self-identified as Black or African American, (2) achieved the superintendency, and (3) able to recall personal experiences as K–12 students
attending segregated schools.

Demographically speaking, the four females and four males ranged
in age from their late 50s to mid-70s and grew up in segregated communities in the midwest, mid-Atlantic, and southern regions of the United States. They were born between 1932 and 1947 and graduated high
school between 1950 and 1965, prior to the implementation of any desegregation plans required by the *Brown II* decision. In fact, half of the
respondents graduated before *Brown* even made it to the Supreme Court.
As such, all but one participant attended segregated schools throughout
her/his entire K–12 years. This participant attended a segregated school
from Grades K–2, but was one of a few Black students who attended elementary and high schools with predominately non-Black populations
from Grades 3–12.

Of the eight superintendents, all earned doctoral degrees in education and demonstrated a personal and professional life committed to
education. For example, while each participant was retired from the
superintendency at the time of this writing, each was still serving in
some capacity within an education-related organization. This includes
positions as university faculty or administrators in educational leadership preparation programs, as well as leadership roles within education
research organizations, systems of higher education, foundations, and
professional associations. All but one earned their undergraduate degrees
at segregated or historically Black colleges and universities (HBCUs), two
earned master's degrees at HBCUs, and all received doctorates at predominately White institutions (PWIs). As superintendents, they were
responsible for districts located in various regions of the country, including the southwest, midwest, mid-Atlantic, northeast, and southeast. Due
to the small number of retired Black school superintendents in the field
who meet the above criteria, pseudonyms are used in this book to preserve their identities, although it should not be assumed that participants
would not be willing to reveal them.

Giving voice to their perspectives, while building on existing and
emergent themes in the research and literature on desegregation, expands
the opportunities and possibilities for improving educational contexts for
historically excluded and marginalized children and communities, which
brings me to the reason for writing this book.

PURPOSE AND OVERVIEW

The negative consequences of school desegregation for Black children, families, and communities in the United States are now well documented in education research. And regardless of one's attitudes concerning the virtues, limits, or problems associated with school desegregation, it is hard to deny the decidedly troubling state of Black education today. This is not to say there are not pockets and examples of great success and educational excellence among Black students in our nation's classrooms and schools, but given the deficit-laden narrative of Black education today and the complex social, economic, and political conditions facing Black and urban communities, no singular work offers clear recommendations for what we must do to ensure student success in these new contexts. This book seeks to fill that void.

Specifically, it aims to critically examine how school desegregation created many of the problems associated with Black education today and why a political race project grounded in racial literacy and led by cross-racial coalitions is needed to advance racial justice, educational equity, and social change in U.S. urban and suburban schools. Historical and contemporary counternarratives to the mainstream depiction of segregated schools and virtues of desegregation ground this work. Scholarship from the fields of education, sociology, political science, law, and Black studies offers the multiple concepts, perspectives, and critiques that inform this line of inquiry. And while it acknowledges the criticisms of critical race scholarship as pessimistic and non-solution-oriented, it seeks to give proper attention to both the realities of racism and hope for meaningful educational change.

Chapter 1 provides an overview of the long-standing debate concerning separate schools, desegregated schools, and equal education. Grounded in Du Bois's question about whether the Negro child should attend separate or mixed schools, this chapter presents the historical, social, and political contexts of schooling for African Americans during segregation and desegregation, with an eye to how this legacy has informed Black education in the 21st century.

While many accounts of all-Black segregated schools focus on what was missing or lacking in these schools, Chapter 2 adds more voices to the rich counternarrative of what school life was like for "Negro" students during segregation. It adds to previous research that documents memories of strict parents, top-notch teachers, encouraging neighbors, and communities that expected nothing less than educational excellence while providing much-needed support within larger racist contexts.

Many Black Americans hoped the *Brown* decision would provide Black children the freedom to attend whatever schools they wanted and would break the stronghold of Jim Crow segregation. Others simply wanted Black schools to have the same resources and educational opportunities as were made available to White schools and children. In Chapter 3, I explore how equalizing educational resources, access, and opportunities took a backseat to achieving racially mixed schools, only to meet hostile resistance from Whites and noncompliance from White-run institutions. I also will discuss the undermining of Black education through the closing of Black schools, demotion and firing of Black educators, and dismantling of the support system enjoyed by Black students and families prior to desegregation.

Chapter 4 will take a closer look at the empty promise of integration through the lens of Derrick Bell's principle of interest convergence, Guinier's conception of interest divergence, and the limits of racial liberalism. It explains not only why meaningful integration did not occur, but also why barriers to desegregation, such as intact busing, resegregated classrooms, and the misappropriation of desegregation funds, were erected to keep Black and White students apart.

Using critical race theory as an interpretive framework for understanding the continued significance of race and racism in U.S. education, Chapter 5 builds on the tradition of Woodson and Du Bois in their focus on race and its role in creating and sustaining inequality in American society. Challenging the myth of a colorblind society and constitution where race is no longer relevant, this chapter emphasizes not only the ways in which race continues to be underestimated in the discourse of school desegregation and related race-conscious laws, policies, and practices, but also why a commitment to abstract concepts of school desegregation, diversity, and inclusion is not enough.

Perhaps most important, Chapter 6 will present recommendations for dismantling what I describe as the *vestiges of desegregation* and delineate a developmental approach to restoring what was lost as a result of the empty promise of integration and what is needed to achieve *equal education* in the future. Embracing the moral activist role of critical race scholarship by identifying strategies and a commitment to praxis, this final chapter puts forth a four-step critical race approach to equal education. I suggest that through a conscious effort to advance racial literacy, racial realism, racial reconstruction, and racial reconciliation in schools and society, we can continue the freedom struggle for equal education in ways that honor the champions of racial and social justice who came before us and would expect us to carry the proverbial torch for freedom through education.

In no way does this book seek to suggest a return to school segregation or to undermine the significance of the *Brown* decision or the decades of struggle that justice-minded individuals engaged in, with the purpose of dismantling the vestiges of segregation. It does, however, attempt to unpack the complex legacy of school desegregation as depicted by the opening quote. In essence, Simone likened our nation's stated commitment to undo the racial inequality it established and perpetuated through segregation as a "joke," or, in other words, "a thing that is ridiculously inadequate" or "a trick played on someone for fun."

For millions of children and parents across the country, access to a quality education remains "ridiculously inadequate," and decades of re-segregation suggest historically disenfranchised communities of color have been tricked into accepting an illusion of progress and inclusion, believing that equal rights and racial justice had come. And although it may be time to reflect and examine why equal educational opportunities remain elusive, now is not the time to give up.

Now is when we must find ways to dismantle the vestiges of segregation and desegregation, learn from our nation's legacy of racial and social injustice in education, and advance the virtues of true integration.

Not ignoring the past but learning from it can effectively realize "a new community founded on a new form of respect and tolerance," where no child will be forced to integrate into or learn in a burning house.

Part I

EDUCATIONAL QUALITY AND INEQUALITY

CHAPTER 1

Neither Separate
Nor Mixed Nor Equal

Theoretically, the Negro needs neither segregated schools nor mixed schools. What he needs is Education. What he must remember is that there is no magic, either in mixed schools or in segregated schools. A mixed school with poor and unsympathetic teachers, with hostile public opinion, and no teaching of truth concerning black folk, is bad. A segregated school with ignorant placeholders, inadequate equipment, poor salaries . . . is equally bad. Other things being equal, the mixed school is the broader, more natural basis for the education of all youth. It gives wider contacts; it inspires greater self-confidence; and suppresses the inferiority complex. But other things are seldom equal.
—W. E. B. Du Bois, *Does the Negro Need Separate Schools?*, 1935

If one race be inferior to the other socially, the constitution of the United States cannot put them upon the same plane.
—Justice Henry Billings Brown, *Plessy v. Ferguson*, 1896

In his oft-quoted essay, "Does the Negro Need Separate Schools?" W. E. B. Du Bois (1935) posed a succinct yet provocative question that remains at the heart of the contemporary debate on school integration. Can Black children in the United States receive a good education in schools designed and intended solely for White children? Moreover, are racially integrated or "mixed schools" (Du Bois, 1935, p. 328) the only means by which Black children can receive a quality education? Supporters of integration and social justice educators alike may reject the premise of Du Bois's question, asserting, as the U.S. Supreme Court did in 1954, "separate educational facilities are inherently unequal" (*Brown v. Board of Education*). Conversely, in that same essay, Du Bois sought to shift our focus from whether a school was racially separate or mixed to whether a school possessed the elements required for a "proper education," which he listed as:

a. sympathetic touch between teacher and pupil;
b. knowledge on the part of the teacher, not simply of the individual taught, but of his surroundings and background, and the history of his class and group;
c. such contact between pupils, and between teacher and pupil, on the basis of perfect social equality, as will increase this sympathy and knowledge;
d. facilities for education in equipment and housing;
e. and the promotion of such extra-curricular activities as will tend to induct the child into life. (p. 328)

Yet more than 70 years after Du Bois (1935) concluded that a proper education was more important than a school's racial composition, and that "to endure bad schools and wrong education because the schools are 'mixed' is a costly if not fatal mistake" (p. 330), questions concerning the virtues, vestiges, and viability of school desegregation remain. Are school integration and racial diversity efforts that require extensive busing and transfer plans due to residential segregation by race more important than providing a quality education in neighborhood schools? Can single-race schools be considered successful and equitable in the post–Civil Rights era?

These inquiries are not centered, in this discussion, on whether legalized segregation should have ended or continued, or whether integrated schools that effectively educate all of their students are most desirable. In my estimation, those matters have been settled. Rather, the question we must ask today, given the persistence of racial prejudice and racism, is very much like that posed by Du Bois in 1935: Do Black Americans (or Latino Americans, or Native Americans, or Asian Americans, etc.) need separate schools to receive a proper education? And if so, are these schools *inherently* unequal?

AN UNEQUAL AND IMPROPER EDUCATION

Sadly, Black education in the 21st century continues to reflect both the racial separation and feelings of inferiority that *Brown* sought to remedy. According to Franklin and Moss (1988):

> It is not possible to measure the effects that separate and unequal education had on both white and black populations in the areas where it was

maintained. Separate schools were doubtless one of the strongest sup-
ports of the concept of white supremacy in the South. Separate schools,
moreover, contributed to the perpetuation of a leadership that was de-
voted not only to the idea of separate education but also to the maintenance of economic and political inequalities between the white and
black populations. (p. 362)

Indeed, the Black–White achievement gap and host of problems that both
contribute to and result from unequal educational opportunities are many.

They include the overrepresentation of Black males in special education (Artiles, 2003; Artiles, Trent, & Palmer, 2004; Dunn, 1968; Noguera,
2008); the isolation or removal of Black males who are perceived as discipline problems (Gordon, Paina, & Keleher, 2000; Noguera, 2008); the
tracking of Black students in low-level classes (Mickelson, 2001; Oakes,
1986; Oakes, Wells, Jones, & Datnow, 1997); the disproportionate number
of Black high school dropouts (Orfield, 2009); and the number of Black
students educated in schools with the least amount of resources and least
experienced teachers (Darling-Hammond, 2004; Kozol, 1991). To add in-
sult to injury, the U.S. Department of Education report, *An Examination
of the Conditions of School Facilities Attended by 10th-Grade Students in 2002*, revealed that "black students were more likely than white students to attend
schools where trash was present on the floor (29 percent vs. 18 percent),
graffiti was present (10 percent vs. 3 percent), and ceilings were in disre-
pair (12 percent vs. 7 percent)" (Alliance for Excellent Education, 2008).

The Black–White Achievement Gap

Even though there is no difference in mental aptitude or intellectual
ability among children of different racial and socioeconomic backgrounds
before reaching 1 year of age, a gap between Black and White students exists in practically every measure and evaluation of academic achievement.
From test scores in reading and math, to high school and college gradu-
ation rates, African American students continue to underperform educationally when compared with their White counterparts. While some have
called into question the tools used to measure educational progress and
achievement, such as IQ tests and standardized testing (Hilliard, 2003;
Sturm & Guinier, 2000; Walters, 2008), the fact that Black seniors in high
school are reading at the same level as White eighth graders is a problem.
In fact, the National Assessment of Educational Progress reported that
88% of Black eighth graders are reading below grade level and that "the
twelfth-grade reading scores of black males were significantly lower than
those for men and women across every other racial and ethnic group."

While 78% of White students graduate from high school, only 55% of Black students graduate, with only 23% of them prepared for postsecondary education. Although to a large extent these data are correlated to income and poverty, far too many Black children raised in middle-class and affluent families also are performing at lower levels than their White and Asian counterparts (Ogbu, 2003). Table 1.1 shows the racial/ethnic enrollment in U.S. public schools.

This Black–White test gap (Jencks & Phillips, 1998) and the more broadly conceptualized "achievement gap" have received overwhelming attention from educators, policymakers, and social commentators alike, and are cause for great concern based on the fact that Black students are not learning or achieving at the same rate as their White peers. Although the gap closed during the 1970s and 1980s, and some integration advocates have attributed that closing to the effects of school desegregation, the problem of Black student underachievement has become a public policy issue resulting in states such as Texas and Georgia launching initiatives to identify ways to increase achievement among African American students, particularly boys.

In 2006, the Schott Foundation, which has conducted extensive research on public education and the Black male, found that school districts with high numbers of Black students are more likely to "have racially segregated schools, do worse on the National Assessment of Educational Progress, suspend and expel more Black boys than White boys, and assign more Black boys than White boys to Special Education using procedures open to abuse and effectively preventing those students from receiving a high school diploma with their peers" (Holzman, 2006, p. iii). In addition to concluding that disproportionate high school dropout, unemployment, and imprisonment rates can be linked to "this widespread, deep, systemic failure to educate African-American males as efficiently as their White counterparts," it also found "that states and most districts with large African-American enrollments can educate some children, but most do not educate the majority of their African-American boys" (p. ii).

The tragedy of the achievement gap truly lies in what we know about the correlations between low reading scores, special education placement, high school dropouts, and unemployment—categories where Black students, especially males, are heavily overrepresented. They pave the pathway to prison. According to the 2007 Children's Defense Fund Cradle to Prison Pipeline® Report,

> The most dangerous place for a child to try to grow up in America is at the intersection of poverty and race. That a Black boy born in 2001 has a 1 in 3 chance and a Latino boy a 1 in 6 chance of going to prison in their

TABLE 1.1. Racial/Ethnic Enrollment in Public Schools

Percentage distribution of the race/ethnicity of public school students enrolled in kindergarten through Grade 12: October 1998–October 2008

Oct.	White	Black	Hispanic	Asian/PI	AI	Two or more races
1998	62.4	17.2	15.4	4.0[1]	1.1	—
1999	61.9	16.5	16.2	4.5[1]	1.0	—
2000	61.3	16.6	16.6	4.2[1]	1.3	—
2001	61.3	16.5	16.6	4.3[1]	1.3	—
2002	60.7	16.5	17.6	4.0[1]	1.2	—
2003	58.3	16.1	18.6	4.0	0.6	2.4
2004	57.4	16.0	19.3	4.1	0.8	2.4
2005	57.6	15.6	19.7	3.9	0.7	2.5
2006	56.9	15.6	20.2	4.0	0.7	2.7
2007	55.9	15.3	20.9	4.4	0.8	2.6
2008	55.5	15.5	21.7	3.9	0.9	2.6

Source. U.S. Department of Commerce, Census Bureau, Current Population Survey (CPS), October Supplement, 1988–2008

lifetime is a national disaster and says to millions of our children and to the world that America's dream is not for all. (p. 4)

Beyond the Black–White Binary: Immigration and Discrimination in Schools

In this book, I have limited my discussion of separate and unequal education to the implications of school segregation and desegregation for Black children, families, schools, and communities. It is not my intent to exclude or further marginalize other groups or communities of color through this focus on African Americans, particularly since the history of discrimination and legacy of exclusion and separation in schools is by no means the sole province of Blacks in the United States (Alvarez, 1986; Olivas, 2006; Takaki; 1993; Tamura, 2008). In fact, the Black–White binary that often frames the historical, legal, political, and social examinations of race, racism, and the law, as well as the more contemporary investigations into the achievement gap, is problematic at best. Thus, my decision to focus on the unequal and improper education of Black students should not be interpreted as an insensitivity to the struggles and experiences of other racial, ethnic, and/or cultural communities, but rather an attempt to explore more deeply the history and lived experiences of one particular group, which I believe can result in important lessons for all.

I do find it critically important to note the historical and contemporary significance of educational discrimination facing Latino, Asian, and Caribbean immigrants in understanding both the legacy and practice of maintaining separate and unequal schools in America. In 2010, the United States is experiencing its largest entry of immigrants, mainly Hispanic and Asian (Orfield, 2009), and we are closer than we have ever been to a majority non-White public school population, although "our two largest minority populations, Latinos and African Americans, are more segregated than they have been since the death of Martin Luther King more than forty years ago" (p. 6).

As the largest growing ethnic population in the United States, Latino children, families, and communities continue to face the discrimination that has plagued them since before the 1931 Lemon Grove incident in Orange County, California. The *Hernandez v. Texas* (1954) decision, which "held that the Fourteenth Amendment protects those beyond the racial classes of white or 'Negro,' and extends to other racial and ethnic groups, such as Mexican Americans," too often has been overlooked. A group that is beginning to garner growing attention in the education research literature is Caribbean immigrants, who effectively and necessarily complicate the racial, cultural, immigrant, and lingual paradigms in which U.S. education traditionally has operated. Arguably, they are not African American. But are they Black? If they speak English, how do we classify them? What if they do not? These questions and more like them will be increasingly significant as to whether or not we consider the role of race in education and how the meaning we ascribe to race informs the educational opportunities provided for and experienced by children.

Resegregation and Within-School Segregation

Although the primary objective of *Brown*, as widely described by the litigants and attorneys who first brought the consortium of desegregation cases to the NAACP, was not to simply "mix bodies" by race, it was argued that desegregated classrooms and schools were essential to the future of positive race relations in not only the schools, but the larger society. Attention to racial balance, however, quickly took precedence over the principal fight for equal resources, and the phenomenon of resegregation was observed and defined as early as 1984 as "a reversal of deseg-regation outcomes where a system or institution, which was previously desegregated, again becomes segregated" (Adair, 1984, p. 186). Less than 10 years later, Eyler, Cook, and Ward (1983) used the same term to de-scribe what they observed in classroom contexts where students were racially or ethnically separated within larger desegregated school set-tings. Furthermore, the association between desegregation and the prac-tice of tracking in schools has been characterized as first-generation and second-generation segregation, respectively (Meier, Stewart, & England, 1989; Welner & Oakes, 1996), whereby first-generation segregation represents district-level segregation and second-generation segregation refers to "the racially correlated allocation of educational opportunities within schools typically accomplished by tracking" (Mickelson, 2001, p. 216. Also referred to as "within-school segregation," these practices of ability grouping and tracking largely result in racially identifiable class-rooms and reproducing educational inequality in terms of resources, cur-riculum, rigor, and thus outcomes (Mickelson & Heath, 1999; Oakes, 1986, 1993, 1995).

Whether a backward slide to segregation or maintenance of racial isolation in desegregated contexts, the goal of meaningful school integra-tion where diverse backgrounds and perspectives are accepted and re-spected remains elusive in most U.S. school systems and communities. Clotfelter, Vigdor, and Ladd's (2006) study of racial isolation in southern school districts attributes perceived increases in resegregation to "the re-sult of demographic change rather than any growing racial imbalance among schools" (p. 381). Orfield (2009), however, contends that racial isolation is worse than ever before, noting that the increasing numbers of non-White schoolchildren as a percentage of our nation's students ex-plain why Whites believe segregation is a thing of the past. "Even as black and Latino students are becoming more isolated, the typical white child is in a school that is more diverse than the school white children attended a generation ago" (p. 26), making it difficult for Whites to recognize how extensive resegregation has become.

The data documenting the degrees of racial isolation, racial imbal-ance, resegregation, and within-school segregation are important to understanding the effectiveness of school desegregation policy, and, in turn, its impact on student learning and achievement. So much that re-searchers on both sides of the desegregation debate could agree that the integration ideal has disintegrated into abstract discussions of diversity, inclusion, and reform. Although more racially, ethnically, and culturally diverse in student composition, U.S. schools and society slowly and quiet-ly have returned to their historical roots of segregation, and, accordingly, the more pressing concern is what this "separateness" means for the goals of educational quality and equality.

IS SEPARATE INHERENTLY UNEQUAL?

According to the *Brown* decision, "separate schools are inherently unequal" and "separate but equal" has no place in the field of education. But what does that really mean? Are all of the schools in homogeneous White communities inherently unequal too? How do we define *separate*? And perhaps more important, how do we conceptualize *equal*?

Defining *Separate* and *Unequal*

Much like Justice Potter Stewart's "I know it when I see it" definition of obscenity, most of us know inequality when we see it. Or do we? While blatant examples of educational inequality are well documented and referenced, more nuanced examples of it represent the challenge associated with ensuring equal educational opportunities for all children. As superintendent of a predominately White, affluent, suburban school district in the South in the 1990s, Dr. Wells, one of the superintendents interviewed for the research study, recalled visiting a school to conduct classroom observations only to witness some practices that "were very disturbing." After observing the White children enjoying reading time lying with their books on the rug and discussing the stories, she noticed the only three Black children in the class were assigned to an adult tutor in the back of the room who was reviewing phonics. So Dr. Wells asked the principal, who was a White woman, "What do you see wrong with this situation . . . with what we see in this class?" The principal didn't notice anything out of the ordinary. So Dr. Wells helped her: "There are three Black kids in this class. Where are they?" After Dr. Wells shared this account, and others like it, she explained that these incidents become "images that stick with you because you know they're so wrong."

But ironically, the principal and classroom teacher were not able to discern this seemingly overt example of inequality. And since the only three Black children were separate from the White children in the class, was this racial segregation? Chief Justice Earl Warren declared school segregation unconstitutional based on social science evidence that showed that separating Black children from White children because of their race "generates a feeling of inferiority as to their status in the community that may affect their hearts and minds in a way unlikely to ever be undone." While we are generally clear as to what separating Black and White children meant in 1954, what do we mean by *separate* today?

Does it matter if the separateness is voluntary or mandated? By which classifications is it appropriate to separate children? Is it okay to separate them by age and gender, but not race or class? While these questions go far beyond the scope of this discussion, I believe they are important to interrogating our understanding of separate, segregated, and the state of segregation that existed in U.S. schools for more than a century. As Ravitch (1980) explicated in "Desegregation: Varieties of Meaning," a book chapter in Derrick Bell's edited collection, *Shades of Brown: New Perspectives on School Desegregation*, the evolving meanings of the terms *segregation* and *desegregation* are semantically significant and offer important clues as to the ways in which desegregation policy would or would not be implemented in relation to the intent and spirit of *Brown*.

For this discussion, I use historian C. Vann Woodward's (1955) definition and explanation of "segregation" as:

> physical distance, not social distance—physical separation of people for reasons of race. Its opposite is not necessarily "integration" as the word is currently used, nor "equality." Nor does the absence of segregation necessarily imply the absence of other types or injustice or the lack of a caste structure of society. . . . Since segregation is subject to the whim of individuals and the custom of localities it could and did crop up in all periods and in numerous manifestations. (pp. xi–xii)

It is important to note Woodward's distinction between segregation and integration (which I presented in greater detail in the Introduction), but also his mention of *equality*. He wants to make sure we are clear that the mere absence of the "physical separation of people for reasons of race" does not allow us to assume equality or justice, as has been the case throughout history. So, then, what is equality?

In the context of school desegregation, the *Brown* decision, according to Guinier (2004), "became the gold standard for defining the terms of formal equality: treating individuals differently based on the color of their skin was constitutionally wrong" (p. 93). Thus, *Brown*, and "the formal equality rule it yielded" (p. 93), led "advocates of color blindness . . . to equate race-conscious government decisions that seek to develop an integrated society with the evils of de jure segregation." This conceptualization of equality not only shifted efforts to advance educational equality by using school desegregation as the end rather than the means to a goal, but it defined equality as "the absence of formal, legal barriers that separate the races" rather than "a fair and just distribution of resources" (p. 95).

Given the various definitions and conceptualizations of *separate* and *equal*, I find that America's dual system of education offers the best starting point for our exploration of what *separate* and *equal* mean in both theory and practice. It underscores how the socially accepted construct of Black inferiority supported and sustained a racially separate and inequitable system (Bell, 2004; *Brown v. Board of Education*, 1954; *Plessy v. Ferguson*, 1896), resulting in lasting implications for the education, socialization, and life chances of Black people for generations to come.

A Legacy of Unequal Education

Since slavery, African Americans have held fast to the belief that access to a quality education would help right the wrongs of a racist past, equating education with opportunity and freedom (Anderson, 1988; Franklin & Moss, 1988). Research literature on the education of Black students has demonstrated how a legacy of educational oppression, both psychological and political, has disadvantaged Black learners (Irvine, 1991; King, 2005; Watkins, 2001; Watkins, Lewis, & Chou, 2001), who continue to experience the long-term effects of the collective mistreatment suffered by their forbears. According to anthropologist John Ogbu (2003), Black children "did not have to have been slaves to internalize the beliefs about the mentality of the slaves; memories of the collective experience of the past influenced their thinking" (p. 80). Thus, the history of separate and unequal is an important feature of American education that cannot be relegated to a past detached from the present or future.

Discussions of school segregation and unequal education are almost always dominated by references to the *Brown* decision of 1954, although issues of race, place, and schooling were acknowledged and contested more than a century earlier in the Massachusetts court case *Roberts v. City of Boston*. In 1848, a Black father by the name of Benjamin Roberts sought to dispute the inequitable treatment his 5-year-old daughter, Sarah, experienced by being forced to "walk through the streets of the city of Boston past five elementary schools for White children to reach the Smith Grammar School, which had been established in 1920 for Blacks." Since the school lacked adequate equipment and was in poor physical condition, Roberts's attorney, Civil Rights leader and later U.S. Senator Charles Sumner, argued that forcing Black children to attend racially separate schools was to "brand a whole race with the stigma of inferiority and degradation" (*Roberts v. City of Boston*, 1848–1849). Despite his argument, which laid an important foundation for the social science research that later would serve as the primary argument in *Brown*, Justice Shaw was not convinced, and "merely asserted that school segregation was for the good of both races." This declaration would introduce the notion of "separate-but-equal," later to be codified in *Plessy v. Ferguson* (1896) and live on for more than a century in spite of the ratification of the Fourteenth Amendment in 1868, which Justice Powell described nearly a century later as "virtually strangled in its infancy by post-Civil War judicial reactionism" (*Regents of the University of California v. Bakke*, 1978).

OUR COLORBLIND CONSTITUTION

Despite the 100-year reign of government-sanctioned racial segregation in U.S. schools and society, *Plessy v. Ferguson* (1896) usually is presented and offered by way of Justice John M. Harlan's lone dissenting opinion, which stated:

> The white race deems itself to be the dominant race in this country. And so it is, in prestige, in achievements, in education, in wealth, and in power. . . . But in view of the constitution, in the eye of the law, there is in this country no superior, dominant, ruling class of citizens. There is no caste. Our constitution is color-blind, and neither knows nor tolerates classes among citizens. In respect of civil rights, all citizens are equal before the law. The humblest is the peer of the most powerful.

And while his lone dissent often is depicted as the "desirable moral standard of the nation" (Alexander & Alexander, 2001, p. 498), it is important to remember the majority opinion offered by Justice Brown and its explicit attack on the Thirteenth and Fourteenth Amendments. Brown's distinction between "political" and "social" equality provides a more accurate picture of how the constitution may have been colorblind, but society was not. He explained:

> Legislation is powerless to eradicate racial instincts or to abolish distinctions based on physical differences, and the attempt to do so can only result in accentuating the differences of the present situation. If the civil and political rights of both races be equal, one cannot be inferior to the other civilly or politically. If one race be inferior to the other socially, the Constitution of the United States cannot put them on the same plane.
> If this be so, it is not by reason of anything found in the act, but solely because the colored race chooses to put that construction upon it. The argument necessarily assumes that if, as has been more than once the case and is not unlikely to be so again, the colored race should become the dominant power in the state legislature, and should enact a law in precisely similar terms, it would thereby relegate the white race to an inferior position. We imagine that the white race, at least, would not acquiesce in this assumption. The argument also assumes that social prejudices may be overcome by legislation, and that equal rights cannot be secured to the negro except by an enforced commingling of the two races. We cannot

accept this proposition. If the two races are to meet upon terms of social
equality, it must be the result of natural affinities, a mutual appreciation
of each other's merits, and a voluntary consent of individuals.

Thus, the Supreme Court determined "the equal protection clause
subject to custom and tradition in accordance with legislative interpretation, no matter how blatantly and objectionably the law affected a particular classification of people" (Alexander & Alexander, 2001, p. 500).
And although *Plessy* did not deal with schools directly, the separate-but-
equal precedent quickly was applied to the field of education. In 1899, the
case of *Cumming v. Board of Education of Richmond County, Georgia* resulted
in a decision by the U.S. Supreme Court that abdicated the school board
from the responsibility of accommodating the needs of Black children by
declaring that how education was carried out was a state issue. In 1908,
the rationale for segregation in education was expanded in *Berea College
v. Kentucky* when the Supreme Court held that a private institution could
not teach Blacks and Whites simultaneously unless the classes were held
no less than 25 miles apart.

Although the cases of *Plessy, Cumming,* and *Berea College* protected
states in their desire to require separate educational institutions and systems for Blacks and Whites, the Court moved beyond the Black–White binary in *Gong Lum v. Rice* (1927) and determined that it was appropriate for
the state to require a Mongolian child to attend its Black school and not its
White school, a practice that became commonplace in both the northern
and southern parts of the country. In 1938, for the first time, the concept
of separate-but-equal was challenged in the case of *Missouri ex rel. Gaines
v. Canada*. The Court deemed unconstitutional a Missouri law prohibit-
ing Blacks from enrolling in the University of Missouri Law School since
there were no in-state alternatives. Not only did the decision signal "a
reassertion of judicial authority in construing the equal protection clause
as a limitation on a previously unfettered state action in education" (Alexander & Alexander, 2001, p. 501), but it also paved the way for *Sweatt
v. Painter* (1950), which essentially did away with racially separate law
schools and posed a serious blow to the doctrine of separate-but-equal.

Nevertheless, Jim Crow segregation continued. And while the *Brown*
decision of 1954 would mark an historic turning point concerning the
separate-but-equal doctrine, several cases post-*Brown* would reflect the
trend Orfield (1996) characterized as "sleepwalking back to Plessy." And
somewhere along the way, "color-blindness replaced equality as the measure of the law" (Minow, 2008, p. 645). In fact, this nightmare would
continue until 2007 and perhaps reach its darkest moment with the *Par-*

ents Involved in Community Schools (2007) decision and Chief Justice John Roberts's declaration that "the way to stop discrimination on the basis of race is to stop discriminating on the basis of race" (pp. 40–41).

THE END OF RACISM?

Indeed, the recurring desire by many to move beyond race to a place of colorblindness (Bonilla-Silva, 2006), or a place where race is neither real nor relevant, continues and has important implications for schooling and education (Anderson, 2007). The election and inauguration of Barack Obama, the first U.S. President of African ancestry, was purported to usher in what some social commentators and colorblind advocates described as a "post-racial era" where race was transcended and racism conquered. But almost as quickly as the term *post-racial* entered the lexicon, meeting great contestation from an even larger number of academics, public intellectuals, journalists, and social critics (Alemán, 2010; Dyson, 2008; Steele, 2008), the post-racial promise was rendered both incongruous and empty. The racially charged rhetoric and discourse that framed and continues to frame the critique and displeasure with President Obama and his administration arguably embody the salience of racism more than our ability to transcend it. Rather, as Dyson (2008) argued, our desire as a nation should not be to transcend race, but rather to transcend racism.

Although the issue of race remains highly controversial, it continues to permeate and influence nearly every aspect of American society. At the start of the 20th century, both Carter G. Woodson and Du Bois "presented cogent arguments for considering race as *the* central construct for understanding inequality" (Ladson-Billings & Tate, 1995, p. 50). Yet, more than a century later, many contemporary discussions and analyses of school desegregation fail to acknowledge the pervasive role of race in desegregation policy specifically and education policy more broadly. According to Guinier (2004), "For a surprising number of blacks, the question is not whether we mistook integration for the promised land," but whether "the promised land can exist in a United States that has yet to come to terms with the way slavery and the racialized compromises it produced shaped our original understanding of the nation as a republic" (p. 97). As an attempt to re-engage race as a construct critical to the examination of inequality in education, I use critical race theory (CRT) in this volume to frame the discussion of school desegregation and the dilemma of whether an equal and proper education can be provided to communities that historically have been excluded and marginalized solely because of race.

An interdisciplinary approach to inquiry, CRT draws from history, law, sociology, philosophy, anthropology, political science, and cultural studies to examine how race and U.S. racial ideology affect and influence legal, political, scientific, and social thought and action in contemporary contexts. By centering race and racism in its analysis, CRT examines the impact and implications of race-conscious policies and practices (e.g., desegregation, school assignment plans, affirmative action in college admissions) and seemingly race-neutral ones (e.g., ability tracking, special education placements, proficiency exams). From its inception in the early 1980s as an intellectual movement led by legal scholars of color, CRT has enjoyed increasing attention as a theoretical framework, methodological tool, and lens of interpretation in education. Ladson-Billings and Tate's (1995) seminal article, "Toward a Critical Race Theory of Education," inspired a wealth of contributions to CRT scholarship in the areas of teacher education, educational leadership, and higher education (Alemán, 2007; DeCuir & Dixson, 2004; Dixson & Rousseau, 2005; Horsford, 2009a, 2009b, 2010a, 2010b; Leonardo, 2005; López, 2003; Parker, 1998, 2003; Parker, Deyhle, & Villenas, 1999; Parker & Villalpondo, 2007; Solórzano & Yosso, 2002; Tate, 1997; Yosso, 2005, 2006). In educational leadership and policy studies, CRT

> serves the dual purpose of providing a race-based interdisciplinary theoretical framework of analysis to the study of education laws, policies, and administrative procedures that have a deleterious impact on racial minorities in K–12 and higher education settings (Roithmayr, 1999). (Parker, 2003, p. 152)

Consequently, education researchers have made important contributions to CRT in education theory and practice by identifying and emphasizing particular themes and tenets representing CRT's foundational principles. In this chapter, I use the five tenets outlined by DeCuir and Dixson (2004): (1) permanence of racism, (2) Whiteness as property, (3) critique of liberalism, (4) interest convergence, and (5) counterstorytelling. See Table 1.2 for definitions of these tenets. Since CRT in education has focused heavily on counterstorytelling and the permanence of racism (see DeCuir & Dixson, 2004), a key feature of this study is the engagement of all five tenets, for which I provide brief descriptions in the following section.

A fundamental tenet of CRT, and often its central criticism, is the *permanence of racism* (Bell, 1992; Crenshaw, 1988). In general, CRT scholars argue that racism, the means by which society allocates status and privilege by race (Delgado & Stefancic, 2001), legitimates perpetual discrimination in American society (Crenshaw, 1988) and is interminable. Based on the salience of racism in U.S. history and jurisprudence, CRT is most concerned with how race is systematically tied to the allocation of social, political, and economic resources (Crenshaw, 1995; DeCuir & Dixson, 2004; Delgado & Stefancic, 2001). Rather than focusing on "blatant acts of hate" or "broad generalizations about another group based on the color of their skin" (López, 2003, pp. 69–70), CRT scholars emphasize how overlooking or ignoring racism's relationship to American hegemony and resource allocation undermines our ability to effectively examine White supremacy and the role of race and power in society and its institutions.

Based on the historical relationship between race, rights, and resource distribution in the United States, the tenet of *Whiteness as property* illustrates how Whiteness, or the right to be *White* as set forth by law, carries with it legal property rights and interests that non-Whites will never be able to enjoy (Harris, 1995). In addition to determining whether a person was "slave or free" (p. 280), "White identity conferred tangible and economically valuable benefits, and it was jealously guarded as a valued possession, allowed only to those who met a strict standard of proof" (p. 280). As such, this inextricable connection between race and property rights in the United States, and more specifically, the value, privilege, and power historically attached to Whiteness, complicates the assumptions that underlie conceptions of equality and fairness under the law.

Accordingly, CRT's *critique of liberalism* takes issue with both conservative and liberal ideological positions that fail to consider race and racism in the examination of laws, policies, and practices and their implications for communities of color (Crenshaw, 1988; Guinier, 2004; Guinier & Torres, 2002; López, 2003; Parker & Villalpondo, 2007). For example, critical race scholars dispute liberal ideals of colorblindness (color or race doesn't matter), meritocracy (access and achievement are based on individual worthiness), and neutrality of the law (all persons are treated equally under the law), all of which conceptualize equality and fairness as the removal of legal racial barriers rather than the equalizing of resources (Guinier, 2004). Thus, a critique of liberal conceptions of race reveals the mythology associated with colorblindness, meritocracy, and equal protection under the law in both theory and practice.

Another consequence of overlooking the endemic nature of race and racism in U.S. law and policy is the phenomenon of *interest convergence*, which describes how the dominant group allows advances for the subordinate group only when and as long as they benefit the dominant group (Bell, 1980a). Using desegregation policy as an example, CRT scholars may argue that administrative practices such as tracking and within-school segregation have been able to persist under the noble banner of desegregation as long as the rights and desires of Blacks (legal right to attend desegregated schools) align with the interests of Whites (ability to have White children not interact with Black children). These racialized structures, hierarchies, and practices demonstrate how race-conscious educational policies that fail to account for race and racism will still advantage the dominant group and continue to disadvantage the group that such remedies arguably were designed to serve.

Despite its emphasis on the systemic reproduction of racial inequality through racialized hierarchies and systems, the experiential knowledge of people of color is also a valued and integral aspect of critical race theory. Through *counterstorytelling*, a foundational precept and methodological tool of CRT, scholars can capture, construct, and reveal marginalized experiences while challenging mainstream narratives that readily may be accepted as objective truths. Telling the stories often left untold, these "personal stories" or "composite stories or narratives" (Solórzano & Yosso, 2002, pp. 32–33) give voice to people, scholars, and communities of color, improving the capacity of educators to better serve historically marginalized or excluded constituencies. As Ladson-Billings and Tate (1995) explained, "Without authentic voices of people of color (as teachers, parents, administrators, students, and community members) it is doubtful that we can say or know anything useful about education in their communities" (p. 58).

CONCLUSION

Unlike Du Bois (1935), who was limited to forecasting, predicting, and anticipating the future of race relations based on "the present attitude of white America toward black America" (p. 328), we have the advantage of retrospection. And while he suggested his contemporaries were mistakenly attempting "to deceive ourselves into thinking that race prejudice in the United States across the Color Line is gradually softening and that slowly but surely we are coming to the time when racial animosities and class lines will be so obliterated that separate schools will be anachronisms" (p. 328), we now know he was right.

But what would Du Bois say about the persistent gaps in education funding, resources, teaching and learning, and achievement across the Color Line in our 21st-century schools? Are these disparities a result of racial prejudice? The failure to provide "the proper education of the Negro race," requiring "sympathetic touch between teacher and pupil; knowledge on the part of the teacher, not simply of the individual taught, but of his surroundings and background, and the history of his class and group"

TABLE 1.2. Tenets of Critical Race Theory

Tenet	Definition
Counterstorytelling	A method of telling a story that aims to cast doubt on the validity of accepted premises or myths, especially ones held by the majority. (Matsuda, 1995)
Critique of liberalism	Critique of basic notions embraced by liberal legal ideology, including colorblindness, meritocracy, and neutrality of the law. (Crenshaw, 1988)
Whiteness as property	Due to the history of race and racism in the United States and the role U.S. jurisprudence has played in reifying conceptions of race, the notion of Whiteness can be considered a property interest. (Harris, 1995)
Interest convergence	Significant progress for Blacks is achieved only when the goals of Blacks are consistent with the needs of Whites. (Bell, 1980, 2004)
Permanence of racism	Racism, both conscious and unconscious, is a permanent component of American life. (Bell, 1992)

(p. 328)? Or was Justice Henry Billings Brown right? That if one race is inferior to the other, there is nothing the government or U.S Constitution can do to make them equal. While the reasons ascribed to the state of unequal and improper education in the United States remain contested, the evidence, sadly, is well substantiated.

What has received less attention in the research literature on school segregation and desegregation are the valued aspects of all-Black segregated schools, which served as safe and caring places where meaningful teaching and learning took place.

• CHAPTER 2 •

A Safe House:
Life in Segregated Schools

As a child of the 1980s, raised in the American southwest, it is difficult for me to imagine going to school, or living life for that matter, in the Jim Crow South. As a Black child raised in a mostly White, but fairly racially diverse working- to middle-class community in southern Nevada, the closest I came to attending a "Black" school was when I was bused to West Las Vegas or the "Westside"—the historically Black side of town for just 1 school year. And since this was part of our school district's mandated desegregation plan, known as the Sixth Grade Center Plan, I was bused for only 1 year for the purposes of desegregating this predominately Black school and maintaining some degree of racial balance across the district.

I share this reflection solely because my understanding of all-Black schools under segregation is limited to the historical research literature I have read and the interviews I have conducted. Before engaging in such research, I believed segregated schools to be nothing more than the unjust products of racism and discrimination. Poorly constructed facilities housing impoverished Black children sitting in inadequately equipped classrooms taught by underprepared Black teachers. And why wouldn't I have imagined this to be so? My understanding was limited to the one-dimensional portrayal of the all-Black school, which, fortunately, has been actively challenged and expanded by historians such as Adam Fairclough and Vanessa Siddle Walker as well as education researchers such as James Anderson and Jerome Morris.

In fact, the past 2 decades have brought forth a growing body of research and counternarratives presented by education researchers, historians, and scholars whose work highlights the valued aspects of segregated schools, providing a more accurate representation of the history of African American education (Anderson, 1988; Jones, 1981; Morris, 1999, 2008; Walker, 1996, 2000). This more fulsome depiction has added greatly to our understanding of all-Black segregated schools, the teachers who taught in them, and the students who learned how to read, write, and succeed in what their elders hoped and expected soon would become a desegregated world. In this chapter, I attempt to contribute to this important body of work by sharing the lived experiences and informed perspectives of selected superintendents as they reflected on their life in segregated schools.

FROM *NEGRO* STUDENT TO *BLACK* SUPERINTENDENT: AN INFORMED PERSPECTIVE

Important research studies have captured the voices and experiences of Black teachers (Beauboeuf-Lafontant, 2002; Dixson & Dingus, 2008; M. Foster, 1997; Ladson-Billings, 1994; Perkins, 1989) and contributions of Black principals (Loder, 2005; Lomotey, 1990; Rodgers, 1967; Tillman, 2004a, 2008; Walker, 1996), but few have investigated the perceptions and perspectives of the Black school superintendent (Horsford, 2007, 2009a, 2010a, 2010b; Hunter & Donahoo, 2005; Moody, 1971; Scott, 1980, 1983) in ways that examine the broad range of concerns and issues faced and addressed by this particular educational leader. The limited scope of scholarship on Black superintendents, whose race becomes central, rather than incidental, to their role as educational experts and leaders in the field, is a missed opportunity in our search for ways to improve Black student achievement in contemporary contexts. Their perspectives are noticeably minimized or altogether absent from the discourse that disproportionately impacts the communities, school systems, families, and children they lead and serve (Morris, 2001; Murtadha & Watts, 2005; Walker, 2000).

For that reason, the analysis of their perspectives, which indeed mirror many of the narratives shared by African Americans who have recounted their segregated schooling experiences, is particularly valuable when using a critical race methodology, which values both their experiential knowledge as people of color and their wisdom of practice as school superintendents leading districts in racialized contexts. While the increasing attention granted to the lived experiences and valued aspects of segregated schools has been criticized by some as selective memory, and others as an "eerie nostalgia" (Guinier, 2004), given the damage and suffering endured during the era of Jim Crow, the extensive and sophisticated professional leadership and network of Black education under segregation are critical to a robust and complete analysis of school desegregation and the successful education of Black children (Walker, 2009).

Table 2.1 presents a demographic profile of the retired superintendents I interviewed for this study. In my interviews, many of the questions I asked them dealt with their identity as "Black" superintendents since one of my many reasons for choosing to interview them was my underlying assumption that their "Blackness" or racial identity granted them a unique and informed perspective on matters of race in education. I also assumed that their self-identifications as Black or African American educational leaders (they all used the terms interchangeably) afforded them experiences and encounters with others who engaged with them in ways that reflected their representation as educational leaders who happened to be Black. I chose to use the term *Negro* in this chapter for much of the same reason James Loewen (2005) did in his book, *Sundown Towns*, as it was "the standard term used to refer to African Americans before about 1972, by black and by whites, and connoted no disrespect" (p. ix.). As stated plainly by participant Dr. Lewis, who was born in 1939, "I grew up Negro, okay, in elementary and middle school. [In the] 1960s, we changed over to Black. I use them interchangeably. [Today] I would be offended by colored or Negro." Despite its contemporary connotation, I use the term in this chapter to locate participant reflections and experiences within their appropriate historical, legal, and social contexts.

Separate Schools, Separate Ways, Separate Worlds

I was surprised to learn of the physical closeness between Blacks and Whites under Jim Crow in many southern towns. When Superintendent Clark reflected on the racially segregated communities in her rural hometown in the South, she acknowledged their close proximity, but characterized them as "separate worlds." She explained that her family "did not live as far away from White people as maybe [I have] in some of the cities where I've lived since then." But despite living in worlds separated by race, she remembered that on occasion, for instance, if somebody died, "there would be some community feeling or acknowledgment . . . you would probably get some attention" from members of the White community. "But other than that, it was separate worlds."

Dr. Marshall lived in a "very small," rural community in the Deep South, which he described as a "small village." A "series of events" led him to a life committed to education. He "started out with an interest in law" because he'd "seen so many injustices that had occurred all over this country." He described farmers losing their land and getting it stolen away from them, as well as the death of Emmett Till, who was murdered not far from where he was raised. Further, he talked about the fact that he had to attend a segregated elementary school and a segregated high school and "was bused to another town to go to a consolidated school away from where we were in the little village that I lived in."

TABLE 2.1. Demographic Profile of Study Superintendents

Name	Born	Sex	Hometown	Education	Superintendency
Baker	1934	F	South, Mid-Atlantic	U–Segregated G–HBCU	Mid-Atlantic
Clark	1934	F	Rural South	U–HBCU G–PWI	West
Cooper	1932	F	Mid-Atlantic, NE	U–Segregated G–PWI	Northeast
Lewis	1939	M	Midwest	U–Segregated G–PWI	Midwest
Marshall	1942	M	South	U–HBCU G–PWI	West, Midwest
Steele	1932	M	South	U–HBCU G–PWI	Midwest
Wells	1947	F	Mid-Atlantic	U–HBCU G–PWI	South
Young*	1942	M	Midwest	U–PWI G–PWI	Northwest, Midwest

* This participant attended segregated schools in Grades K–2 only, but resided in an all-Black segregated community from K–12.

Dr. Baker said she "recognized early on that the only way I could change my condition in life would be to get an education," which also helped shape her desire to help children and become an educator.

Dr. Clark navigated the realities of racial segregation during her formative years with the support of her parents, who helped her to understand, but refrain from internalizing, that reality.

> If your parents were like my parents, they protected you from all of that kind of stuff. You had a good time. You were happy, and so that didn't bother you. You just knew it was there. You knew that you couldn't do certain things. You knew that you had to be careful about certain things, and so on. But other than that, it was not something you went around thinking about

every day. You had your own friends and everything and you had a good time, and it was like any other situation. Going to school, football games, and so forth. It was just with your folk, not them.

Dr. Steele didn't need his parents to explain to him the unspoken norms of racial segregation in the South. He recalled "hearing White politicians talking about how they're going to keep the race pure. And telling poor White folks, 'I don't care how bad off you are, you're better than a nigger.' I cannot and I don't want to forget those experiences." While he remembered the anguish and anger he felt concerning the overt and unforgiving racism he and his siblings experienced as children, he spent more time attributing his personal and professional successes to the support of his community. Dr. Clark also enjoyed a culture of connectedness and collective responsibility within her small, southern Black community, "where the whole community raised you whether they knew you or not." She said that someone didn't have to know you to tell your parents that you were doing something wrong, and "they didn't feel reluctant to tell you that." And most important, "your parents would certainly support them."

Going to School

But nearly all of the participants did have to leave their own community to go to school. In fact, going to school often required traveling long distances past White schools, which was a common experience shared by nearly all the participants. Whether they got there by foot, ferry, or bus, getting to school each day was a racialized experience for each respondent, most of whom could recount with great detail their journey to and from their segregated school. For example, born in 1932, Dr. Steele was able to list and describe every street he walked and the number and type of White schools he passed to get to his all-Black elementary and high schools.

Dr. Wells also passed by White schools during a long commute to her Black elementary school and high school. Although she lived in a predominately White and dispersed county in the South, there was just one Black elementary school and one Black high school, which required she travel roughly 20 miles each day, passing White schools to get there. Dr. Clark also remembered having a "pretty good distance to walk to school," passing White kids who were headed in the opposite direction. "They'd be going this way, and we'd be going that way, and of course we'd call each other names and stuff like that."

In addition to the physical burden of traveling far distances past White schools to attend their Black schools, societal restrictions limited their access to learning. As a high school student, Dr. Clark could not enter her public library during regular hours because she was *Negro*.

> In doing a lot of my research and writing essays and papers and things . . . I got to go to the public library once it was closed. When they closed the public library for the day, then I got a chance to go to do some of my research there. So that sort of stands out for me.

And while societal restrictions, unjust and unfair treatment, were an everyday reality of students growing up under segregation, participants talked considerably more about the expectations of their parents, teachers, and their community members, all of whom they credit for what they were able to accomplish in what would become a desegregated world.

BLACK SCHOOLS AS PILLARS OF STRENGTH

In Jerome Morris's 1999 article, "A Pillar of Strength: An African American School's Communal Bonds with Families and Community Since *Brown*," the author's conception of *communal bonds* embodies how "all-Black schools historically involved African American families in the affairs of the school as well as functioned as stabilizing institutions for African American communities" (p. 602). There was "shared participation and ownership" among educators, parents, and community members, and the school was embedded within and interdependent with the Black community. These bonds existed between the schools and their communities as well as among the schools' students, teachers, and principals. In fact, much of the research literature on all-Black schools captures the communal bonds, collective work, and caring that characterize the type of safe, supportive, learning environment that many Negro students enjoyed pre-*Brown*. In his extensive study of Black teachers in the South from emancipation to desegregation, historian Adam Fairclough (2004) described Black schools as "places where order prevailed, where teachers commanded respect, and where parents supported the teachers." He also discovered that throughout this period of history in education, "teachers, pupils, and parents formed an organic community that treated schooling as a collective responsibility" (p. 3).

To date, the most comprehensive assessment of research on Black segregated schools is offered by Vanessa Siddle Walker (2000), whose review of education research on the "consistent characteristics" of segregated schools found their valued aspects to be: (1) exemplary teachers, (2) curriculum and extracurricular activities, (3) parental support, and (4) leadership of the school principal. These themes were consistent in my discussion with the selected superintendents; however, due to limited data supporting the aspects of curriculum and extracurricular activities, I present my research findings according to the reflections that emphasized the role and influence of teachers and parents.

Exemplary Teachers

Participant Dr. Cooper attended schools in the mid-Atlantic and remembered Black teachers having "a great deal of authority at that time." They would do whatever was necessary to ensure their students performed to a high standard and they possessed a degree of resolve and respect that is not as prevalent among today's teachers.

> Some folks would allege that they had more authority to demand high performance. Maybe to some extent that may be true because, you know, you were going to be there. If you got kept until midnight, you were going to stay there and do the work . . . there weren't as many options, and teaching was looked upon as a rather noble profession. I think teachers felt that they were respected and admired and trusted, so they brought to that job a level or feeling of commitment and appreciation that some teachers now say they don't think they have.

She continued, "Many of these teachers had been there for years and knew their content. They had the combination of content and pedagogy. These people knew how to teach." Dr. Cooper perceived the extensive experience in subject matter and instruction and the "stability" offered by her teachers as important to her success as a student. Dr. Clark also spoke of two teachers in particular who taught her the fundamental academic and social skills that she credits for preparing her to succeed in high school and beyond. Likewise, Dr. Lewis remembered his segregated schools as being "good" because of the quality of the teachers. According to him, his Black teachers demonstrated wisdom and experience, were visible and involved with the local Black church and community, held high expectations for their students, and were willing to provide additional support even beyond the regular school day and school site.

The memories and images of the Black teacher in segregated schools, as shared by the superintendents, support Walker's (2000) portrait of African American teachers of that era:

Professional educators steeped in an understanding of philosophies about children and teaching, but also committed to their own set of beliefs about how the children should be motivated to achieve. . . . In doing so, they developed a cultural teaching style that assumed their children would be, and must be, taught the curriculum available at White schools, but that also assumed that the students must be motivated to believe that they could achieve and be held accountable for learning. This task they appear to have embraced in their construction of what it meant to be a teacher. (p. 267)

This tradition of great expectations for excellence in Black education was recounted many times over in my interviews with former superintendents, a few of whom still remembered the names of their elementary school teachers. They described their teachers as highly educated and professional, demanding yet caring, and possessing high standards for good behavior and academic achievement from all their students.

Parental Support

While evidence concerning the role of teachers in segregated schools is fairly consistent, this is not the case concerning the role of African American parents in the same contexts. Walker (2000) presents examples of parental support through: (1) financial contributions, (2) advocacy, (3) attendance, and (4) the complementary reinforcement of community values, with the caveat that "the activity attributed to African American parents during this era does not imply consistency in attitudes and beliefs" (p. 273). Much of the dissension and disagreement correlated with the changing needs of the Black school and community.

According to the participants, their parents, family structure, and home life played a critical role in developing their attitudes, philosophies, and experiences concerning education. The values, childrearing styles, and expectations of their parents and guardians contributed to their success, while their race, class, and the education level of their parents seemingly did not have as great an impact on their learning and academic success. In fact, all but two participants described themselves as growing up in very poor to relatively poor households, while two participants grew up in working- to middle-class homes. Two had parents who did not finish high school, five had at least one parent who did finish school, three had parents who received some college education, and one participant had parents who were college graduates. Dr. Wells remembered her parents instilling "strong values around education." She added, "The expectation was that everybody—all of us—would go to college." The question was not *if* you were going to college, but *where* you were going to college.

Dr. Cooper also "came out of a household where there was no expectation not to perform." Her parents, high school graduates who were not able to attend college for financial reasons, raised her in a middle-class home where she always received much support and encouragement. Even as a young, Black female who had limited opportunities based on societal norms that discriminated by race and gender, she recalled, "My father always encouraged me to do whatever I wanted to do." Born to two college graduates and into a family of educators, Dr. Steele described his family as "poor as hell" in relation to their White counterparts. Although his father was a Jeanes Supervisor of Schools and his mother a teacher who later pursued a career in nursing, the family of 10 didn't have much money, causing his father to be teased for where he did choose to spend his resources. As Dr. Steele remembered it, "We might not have any food in the house, but we had books." And while all participants were raised with limited resources and many were children of parents with limited formal education, their parents sacrificed what they did have and compensated for what they may not have had with great expectations for academic excellence and educational success as the necessary preparation for what would become a desegregated world.

PREPARING STUDENTS FOR THE *WHITE* WORLD

While some may argue that desegregation efforts that do not result in integration seem like a step back to "separate-but-equal," Derrick Bell (2004) observed that "some Black educators, however, see major educational benefits in schools where Black children, parents, and teachers can utilize the real cultural strengths of the Black community to overcome the many barriers to educational achievement" (p. 26). Cultural affirmation was important to countering society's assumptions that Blacks were unequal and inferior to Whites, particularly in regard to academic ability. A common response that emerged among participants was the importance of the ability to compete with Whites and succeed. They often spoke of the fact that they did not require any remediation once they left their all-Black segregated schools for postsecondary institutions, and those who attended graduate school at predominately White institutions discovered or reaffirmed that they were just as smart as or smarter than their White counterparts.

And while Dr. Young recalls his parents teaching him to "think above color" and "not to carry a chip on your shoulder because it wasn't going to do you any good," Dr. Baker pointed out that the strategy for coping with racism is to remember that although it is "your reality," it is "not your problem," since you can't change it even if you wanted to. The oral histories and personal testimonies of Black educators and students about their educational experiences under segregation illustrate how Black schools prepared students to "compete in the desegregated world that did not yet exist" (Walker, 2001, p. 769).

The Black Community: Support and Refuge

Support and encouragement were important to the ways participants explained their subsequent personal and professional success. Dr. Steele attributed his being where he is today to the support of his neighbors and local Black community in the South, where "there were people who believed in me." He recalled "people who could not read nor write in [my] neighborhood," but believed in him and were willing to loan what little money they had to his mother to ensure he and his brothers could attend school. He said "they were just as proud of our achievement as they were their own . . . [even] if they didn't have any [achievements]."

Dr. Baker noted that education was critical to African Americans and "recognized early on that the only way I could change my condition in life would be to get an education." She added, "[I] knew that if I didn't get an education I'd be working in some job that I would hate." This was a message sent from her parents, experiences, and people in the community, who "expected that students who performed well would go to college" and "make something out of your life." She laughed, "I mean, everybody did, even the drunks on the corner." Dr. Clark enjoyed that same sense of support and expectation to succeed educationally within her small, rural, southern Black community. She explained that in those days, "the whole community raised you whether they knew you or not," so that even if a person in the community did not personally know who you were, "if they saw you doing something wrong, they didn't feel reluctant to tell you that, and your parents would certainly support them." Also raised in a very small, rural community in the Deep South, Dr. Marshall explained, "If you didn't go to church on Sunday, people would be at your house, wondering what happened to you." It was not uncommon for neighbors and community members within his all-Black community to be tight-knit, involved, and concerned for one another's well-being. Similarly, Dr. Lewis recalled the sense of community that was simply a part of his normal, everyday life in his midwestern all-Black segregated community, which had "everything that you needed—the movies, the barbershop, the cleaners—all that was in [the Village]. So you really didn't have to go outside [the Village] for your needs."

The Black Parent: Involvement and Sacrifice

While all of the superintendents discussed the great support and encouragement they received within their segregated communities, they spoke at length about how their home life played a critical role in the development of their experiences and philosophies concerning education. For these African American families, the role and influence of parents were instrumental to the social-emotional and educational development of the children (Tillman, 2004a). Specifically, their parents' or grandparents' values, childrearing styles, as well as their own relationships with schoolteachers played a large role in their ability to succeed in school. All described their parents' no-nonsense approach to excellence in education as a guiding force that shaped their ability to succeed despite a racist and hostile society. Although the educational background of parents and families ranged from a sixth-grade education to graduate school, the demonstration of sacrifice and unwavering support by parents in ensuring their children took their education seriously was the standard. In fact, the conditions that seemingly did not have as much impact on their ability to learn and achieve academic success, as many would argue today, were the socioeconomic status and/or education level of their parents.

Dr. Lewis recalled how his parents emphasized the importance of education to their five children through word, deed, and the sacrifices they made when faced with difficult decisions on how they would spend their limited resources. In addition, his mother "always used to say she didn't have much education, but she had mother wit, and she used it to the best of her ability . . . she never used the word *excellence*, but in my mind that's what she was telling us. You have to be excellent." Dr. Clark portrayed her parents, neither of whom had a high school education, as being "not all that involved," because they didn't attend PTA meetings, although they had "definite rules to obey and things to do," "went to school activities," and established "a clear understanding between [themselves] and teachers that the support was there." L. Foster (2005) explained that this type of parental involvement, "by historical and traditional imperatives ingrained within the African American community, was to be depended upon to set the tone by which students were conditioned for learning in school" (p. 693). In their study of the segregated schooling of Blacks in the U.S. South and South Africa, Walker and Archung (2003) observed that parents:

> Taught attitudes at home about how teachers were to be treated and
> how students were to conduct themselves at school. Moreover, they in-

stilled in students an understanding of the need for education and provided the time for students to do homework, even though they seldom
helped directly with homework. (p. 32)

Thus, the notion of parental involvement is conceptualized and defined in various ways throughout the collection of narratives. While Dr.
Clark did not consider her parents' high expectations, rigid rules for behavior, and relationship with teachers as parental involvement, Dr. Lewis
believed his parents' mere presence and demonstrated value of education
constituted what some may not identify as parental involvement. Further, Dr. Steele recalled his mother's dual role of setting high standards
and expectations for her children, while also ensuring they were treated
fairly by others. "My mother used to tell us she didn't want anybody low-
ering the standards for us, but she damn sure didn't want nobody raising
the standards on us either."

These narratives illustrate the diversity of African American families, representing a range of socioeconomic conditions (mainly poor and
working class), but sufficiently equipped to ensure their children would
succeed in school. They gave their children literature and exposed them
to materials that helped them to obtain the education the families held in
such high regard. Although the superintendents were Black, had meager
resources, and were children of parents who were not always high school
or college graduates, they were not culturally deprived, living a culture
of poverty, or part of a deficit model. They used their limited resources
to overcome and advance the next generation. Teachers also reinforced
these values.

The Black Teacher: Authority and Advocacy

Participant responses describing the qualifications, role, and influence
of their Black teachers in segregated schools were very similar to the historical accounts found in the related literature. All respondents valued
the role of the Black teacher and expressed regret for the loss of what
they perceived to be an extremely important variable in the education
and achievement of Black students. As Fairclough (2004) observed in his
article, "The Costs of *Brown*: Black Teachers and School Integration," "The
notion that integration destroyed something uniquely valuable to African
Americans in the South has been powerfully influenced by memories of
and about black teachers" (p. 2).

The reflections of these superintendents were strikingly similar. Dr.
Steele remembered his school as having "the best teachers you could find"

because they "knew and believed in our educability and that we were going to be somebody." Although Dr. Clark's school in the South was small, with several grades in one classroom, students were expected to achieve according to their ability. She described her teachers as "excellent advocates, motivators, and leaders," with great influence over the lives of students, who "insisted on excellence in certain areas." She recalled the personalized support students received from teachers beyond academics.

> One of the things about going to Black schools, particularly in the
> South, was that there were no counselors, so if anybody was going to counsel you, it was because another teacher took you under her wings and sort of made sure that you did the right thing.

Similarly, Dr. Baker remembered having "good teachers all the time" who went to top-notch graduate schools, genuinely "cared about education," and were "wonderful influences." Dr. Lewis also recalled his segregated schools as being "good" and explained that it was because of the quality of his teachers whom he described as "excellent" and the "talented tenth."

After I explored further to understand why he believed these teachers were "excellent," he explained that in addition to having graduated in the top 10% of their class (a requirement in order to attend the all-Black teachers college in his hometown), they demonstrated the care they had for their students "by taking time with you in and out of school," "the wisdom they shared," "the extra help they gave you," and "the encouragement." He gave a specific example of his second semester in ninth grade. Despite getting As in every other class, he received a C in algebra and cried to his teacher about the grade. She explained to him that she couldn't "give you what you didn't earn, but if you want to learn algebra, I'll teach it to you." That's the kind of caring he was talking about. "Someone who cared enough to say, 'Okay, you don't know it now, but I'll work with you, and I'll teach you.'"

He also recalled the fact that his teachers often lived in the same neighborhood and attended the same church as their students. Dr. Clark, who frequented church as a child, said that "it wasn't unusual that you would find teachers in your church, in the community . . . so sometimes you would bump into your teacher with your parents . . . that kind of relationship was there."

Dr. Lewis's characterization of the Black teachers who taught in his segregated schools captured many facets of what participants described as important to being a "good teacher." They demonstrated wisdom and experience, were visible and involved in the local Black church and community, expected excellence and possessed high expectations for their students, and were willing to provide additional support even beyond the regular school day. Although Dr. Clark was unsure about the formal education and professional qualifications of the teachers in her rural segregated elementary school, she believed that any possible deficiencies likely were outweighed by the teachers' care and commitment to their students.

> As far as the teachers are concerned, I don't know whether those [White] teachers were better than ours. They possibly were in that some [Black schools] were not as careful about credentialing and making sure that people were teaching in their fields, and so forth, as they possibly were in others. But our teachers were very caring and demanding people and so it probably made up for some things that you might have gotten otherwise.

Fairclough (2004) documented the same sentiment from former students of segregated schools who "have testified to the commitment and skill that those men and women brought to the classroom in the era of Jim Crow" (p. 3). They remembered segregation as encouraging "a special sense of dedication in black teachers that helped compensate for the material deficiencies of the schools" (p. 3).

This notion of the "commanding" and "demanding" teacher also emerged as a common thread among the respondents. The emphasis by teachers on behavior and discipline was indicated repeatedly, and usually tempered with a discussion of how this demonstrated a teacher's "commitment" to and "caring" for students. Many of them spoke of how their teachers would expect the best and accept nothing less, or, as Dr. Baker described it, they "did not take any foolishness off you." Dr. Steele explained the importance of the positive reinforcement and efficacy demonstrated by Black teachers to their Black students within the segregated classroom setting. "You had teachers who said, 'You're going to be something, boy. You're going to learn before you get out of this room.'"

The Black Student: Young, Gifted, and Negro

In addition to the community support system that was available to the participants as young, Negro students living in segregated communities and attending segregated schools, their parents and teachers played a significant role in what they perceived to be their strong self-concept as Black Americans. Supported by institutional caring and interpersonal caring (Walker & Archung, 2003), and recognizing the quality and "goodness" of their Black teachers and schools, participants countered the assumption that an all-Black school is inherently bad, deficient, or inferior. Dr. Steele took issue with the argument that racially isolated Black schools should not exist because their failure is inevitable, unlike all-White schools, which need desegregation only to benefit from exposure to *diversity*. He explained, "There is nothing wrong with something being all-Black. But people will have you think there's something wrong. You know, this country and this world would be in a hell of a fix if we didn't have some of the people that have been produced by those HBCUs."

Dr. Baker, who attended a segregated college and HBCU for her graduate studies, shared what it meant to be a Negro child growing up in a segregated environment.

> That you're smart. That you can do anything you want to do.
> And I must have been dumb enough to believe it [laughing].
> And when your family is telling you that, your school is telling
> you, your church is telling you, hey. They must have it right!

Despite how others may have prejudged her academic ability based on her race, Dr. Wells said she "never felt inferior" and always felt "as smart and capable as any White person." She admitted that "there have been times where things have happened—today they happen—that could shake that confidence if you actually didn't have a strong foundation on which to build." However, the support she received from her family, school, and community greatly influenced her ability to succeed as a Negro student and Black superintendent in both segregated and desegregated educational and professional contexts. Similarly, Dr. Clark's self-concept and academic ability were reaffirmed when she attended graduate school at a predominately White institution in the western region of the United States. "It's something that I have noticed, that many of the graduates of historically Black schools who do well, do well in any environment."

In reflecting upon her life in segregated schools, Dr. Clark said there were features of segregation that she couldn't "pinpoint," but that "seem to have worked for us." After speaking about the high expectations and caring nature of parents and teachers, and the connections they shared as advocates for education, she concluded, "Somehow you wish you could transplant that to [contemporary] environments, because I don't think it is as strong today—and probably not as strong for a lot of reasons because society has changed a great deal."

CONCLUSION

These individual stories contribute to the growing counternarrative of valued segregated schools, which historically have served as pillars of strength in the African American community. This sense of community established through the shared roles and responsibilities for the educational success of Black children by parents, teachers, and community members not only helped to build a support system for students, but also provided the high expectations, financial contributions, advocacy, and leadership necessary to succeed in a racially segregated and hostile world. Through exemplary teachers, parental support, and strong principal leadership, the all-Black segregated school typified the school–family–community linkages and relationships that some educational leaders strive to reclaim in 21st-century schools. These narratives not only challenge notions of genetic inferiority, cultural deprivation, and underachievement among Black students, but bring much-needed attention to the valued, consistent, and affirmative features of all-Black schooling, which made the school a safe house from the psychological harm and physical danger that was a part of the students' everyday world.

As one woman reflecting on the struggle for equal education through school desegregation (see Bell, 2004) put it,

"We got what we fought for, but we lost what we had."

Part II

THE
IDEOLOGY OF
INTEGRATION

• CHAPTER 3 •

Integration and
Interest Convergence

The freedom struggle for equal education through integration was a logical approach to dismantling government-sanctioned segregation in the United States. Those who fought and advocated for the end of racial inequality through integrated schools and society believed removing such legal barriers to equal access, opportunities, and resources, especially in education, would usher in an era of social change, and at last reflect America's reputation as a democratic nation that valued freedom, fraternity, and equality for all her citizens.

Sadly, many of these same individuals have witnessed what they deemed surmountable challenges become seemingly insurmountable odds as racial inequality continues to manifest itself throughout many, if not all, aspects of American life. The racial antagonism and animus that fueled American slavery, the Black Codes, Jim Crow, and other forms of post-slavery racism and discrimination, would continue to limit the ability of Black citizens to dream the American dream with any hopes of its actualization. Given the luxury of hindsight and the embedded nature of U.S. racism, not only was the promise of school integration broken, it was arguably empty, causing further damage through an illusion of progress and inclusion that later would undermine the ability of Blacks to benefit from full participation in American life. As the venerable historian John Hope Franklin suggested, "Perhaps racial integration has failed because it has barely been tried" (Cashin, 2004, p. 23).

This chapter seeks to contextualize the era of segregated schools with a brief discussion of Jim Crow segregation and the social and political conditions that culminated in the *Oliver Brown v. Board of Education of Topeka, Kansas* case of 1954. It is not an exhaustive account of the events or policies that occurred during this period, but rather a discussion of the values and ideologies that framed the goal of integration and the resistance of this ideal due to its reliance on White support, institutions, and approval (Bell, 2004; Walters, 2008).

FROM JIM CROW TO OLIVER BROWN

While the era of Jim Crow segregation in the United States has been well documented by historians, social scientists, and legal scholars, and the term *Jim Crow* commonly used to depict a separation of the races or a racial caste system, those of us who did not live during this time or in this space may never fully know what it was like. We have seen the black-and-white photographs of water fountains labeled "whites only" and "coloreds only," and are familiar with the practice of Blacks riding in the back of the bus or denied entry into White restaurants, hotels, and theaters, but to internalize the psychological and spiritual damage that such a system perpetuates probably is elusive for those who were not there. In his discussion of slavery and post-slavery forms of discrimination and oppression, Walters (2008) explained, "This process of dehumanization is important as a preliminary step to the attendant process of subordination and has been an interactive variable with subordination at every step of American history and the hidden justifier of oppressive acts against Blacks" (p. 85). While we often speak of Jim Crow as a system of law, a way of life, and an era of American history, many unanswered questions remain. Who was Jim Crow anyway? And why did he insist on the separation of the races?

In C. Vann Woodward's book, *The Strange Career of Jim Crow* (1955), which Dr. Martin Luther King, Jr., described as the Bible of the Civil Rights movement, Woodward attempts to explain the origins of the term and its application to Blacks, which he characterized as "lost in obscurity" (p. 7). According to Woodward, "Some historians have concluded that the full-blown Jim Crow system sprang up immediately after the end of slavery to take the place of the Peculiar Institution" (p. 25). While he discovered the first mention of Jim Crow in 1832 as the name of a song and dance written by Thomas D. Rice, the term "had become an adjective by 1838" and "used by writers in the 1890's" (p. 7). Franklin and Moss (1988) record Tennessee as passing the first Jim Crow law in 1875, with all other southern states quickly following suit.

These "segregation statutes" (Woodward, 1955, p. 7) separated the races in both public and private places, and effectively prohibited Blacks from White venues after the U.S. Supreme Court in 1883 banned the Civil Rights Acts of 1875 (Franklin & Moss, 1988). Just 2 years later, racially segregated schools became the order of the day in the South, a system to be sanctioned in 1896 in *Plessy v. Ferguson*, "a further action against the citizenship of Blacks that merely codified the various forms of racial subordination already being perpetrated against them in the South and in other parts of the country" (Walters, 2008, p. 90). Clearly, this maintenance of a dual education system was costly; however, "the expense of maintaining a double system of schools and other public institutions was high, but not too high for advocates of white supremacy, who kept the races apart in order to maintain things as they were" (Franklin & Moss, 1988, p. 238).

The South, however, was in no way the only region that practiced forms of Jim Crow segregation. Discussions and analyses of U.S. segregation often have focused on southern states because of their official policy of segregation (Clotfelter, Vigdor, & Ladd, 2006). However, a growing body of research literature on segregation and desegregation in the North (Guinier, 2004; Sugrue, 2008) and West (Horsford, 2008) is expanding our understanding of the "strange career of Jim Crow" and its national impact. Woodward (1955) highlighted these regional distinctions using the words of French politician and historian Alexis de Tocqueville, who "was amazed at the depth of racial bias he encountered in the North" (p. 20). "'The prejudice of race,' he wrote, 'appears to be stronger in the states that have abolished slavery than in those where it still exists; and nowhere is it so intolerant as in those states were servitude has never been known'" (p. 20).

Interestingly, Tocqueville's field notes in fact may capture the basis of segregationist and former South Carolina Governor and U.S. Senator Strom Thurmond's preference for southern-style segregation. The former presidential candidate explained, "Segregation in the South is honest, open and aboveboard. Of the two systems, or styles of segregation, the Northern and the Southern, there is no doubt whatever in my mind which is the better." While systems of racial prejudice, discrimination, and inequality were not limited to the Jim Crow South, they were able to sustain themselves throughout the nation given the consent and support of the federal government.

Thurmond's penchant for the South's "honest" brand of segregation was shared by President Woodrow Wilson, who in 1913 appointed segregationists to federal offices "because of his firm belief that racial segregation was in the best interest of Black Americans and White Americans alike" (*The Rise and Fall of Jim Crow*, 2010). Indeed, "the trend in the North . . . was toward the adoption of the Southern Way as the American Way" (Woodward, 1955, p. 113). The early 1900s also marked the emergence of the National Association for the Advancement of Colored People (NAACP), National Urban League, Black Greek-Letter organizations on college campuses, church leaders and their congregations, and many individual activists dedicated to the cause of equal rights and social justice (Jackson, 2008). Voting rights, equal employment rights, fair housing, health care, and the quest for equality in all areas of American life were challenged, but the most important issue, second to voting, was the right to an equal education (Jackson, 2008).

WHY *BROWN* HAPPENED *WHEN* IT HAPPENED

After 100 years of "separate-but-equal" in the United States, what led to the unanimous *Brown* decision of 1954? After the decades of precedent firmly established in the law concerning the separation of the races as "good for both races," what made the Court ignore these prior cases and deem "separate schools as inherently unequal" in the eyes of the law? Was desegregation, or even integration, an idea whose time had finally come? As with all social movements, political victories, and social change, timing was everything, and as Jackson (2008) explained, the education strategists knew that in order to win, "the timing had to be right" (p. 137).

But while some scholars credit societal progress, and a readiness on the part of Americans to at last grant civil rights to all of its citizens, for the *Brown* decision, many variables, both foreign and domestic, played important roles that paved the road to the dismantling of the doctrine of separate-but-equal. For example, after defending America in World War I, many Blacks returned home with "a new hope for restoration of their rights and a new militancy in demanding first-class citizenship" (Woodward, 1955, p. 114). As a result, in 1919, there were 25 race riots throughout the country, including places such as Longview, Texas; Tulsa, Oklahoma; Knoxville, Tennessee; and Chicago, Illinois (Woodward, 1955). Black Americans were lynched in uniform, the southern brand of racism and segregation was becoming more explicit in the North, and the Ku Klux Klan was established in Georgia in 1915, spreading "racism in regimented form" throughout the 1920s and across the country (Woodward, 1955).

As racial tensions decreased during the 1930s, with the Great Depression, and the hardship it placed on both Blacks and Whites, segregation law was expanded. At the same time, the federal government, and President Roosevelt's New Deal, sought to extend access and opportunities for Blacks in the areas of housing, health, and education. During this decade, Charles Hamilton Houston, dean of Howard University Law School, was in the process of not only transforming his law school, but also advancing the fight for racial justice. Houston "urged African Americans to undergo the rigors of intense legal training so that they might join the fight to secure for an entire race real equality under the law" (Ogletree, 2004, p. 116).

Houston's strategic approach to preparing civil rights attorneys would be critical to the primary fight to eliminate segregated education, which was being challenged at the graduate level. The *Missouri ex rel. Gaines v. Canada* case of 1935 required that each state "provide education for all its citizens and the provision must be made *within the state*," declaring that "the provision for the payment of tuition fees in another State does not remove the discrimination" (Franklin & Moss, 1988, p. 365). Despite the legal progress made concerning equal opportunities for Blacks in higher education, by the early 1950s, "both the friends and foes of segregation in education conceded that the bitter fight would be waged on the level of the elementary and secondary schools, and the fight was not long in coming" (Franklin & Moss, p. 366). In an effort to preserve *separate-but-equal*, segregationists worked to maintain racially separate schools by investing state funds to bring Negro schools up to par with White schools. In many cases, southern states quickly built new Black schools to avoid the mixing of the races, so that "within a few years some of the most modern schools to be found anywhere in the United States had been constructed for Negro children in Southern communities" (Franklin & Moss, 1988, p. 366).

This maneuvering by southern leaders compelled the NAACP "to attack the very principle of segregation as unconstitutional," and in 1952, took the issue of segregated schools to the U.S. Supreme Court (Franklin & Moss, 1988, p. 366). The NAACP's group of litigants representing cases in Virginia, South Carolina, Delaware, Washington, D.C., and, most notably, Topeka, Kansas, successfully argued their case, and the Court unanimously concluded that segregation did not belong in education and that "separate educational facilities are inherently unequal" (*Brown v. Board of Education*, 1954). It determined that "state laws permitting and requiring such segregation, denies to Negro children the equal protection of the laws guaranteed by the Fourteenth Amendment—even though the physical facilities and other 'tangible' factors of white and Negro school may be equal" (*Brown v. Board of Education*).

But how did the Court come to such a conclusion in light of the staunch resistance that remained in the South by citizens and politicians alike? Perhaps the attorney general's support of the NAACP's position on school segregation and declaration that "racial discrimination furnishes grist for the Communist propaganda mills, and it raises doubt even among friendly nations as to the intensity of our devotion to the democratic faith," grant us some insight into how other prevailing interests influenced why *Brown* happened when it did (Franklin & Moss, 1988, p. 366).

When Interests Converge

"The interests of blacks are only realized when they converge with the interest of whites," according to legal scholar Derrick Bell, who in his book *Silent Covenants* (2004) questioned the altruistic motivation behind *Brown*. Bell argued the case is an example of his principle of *interest convergence*, the phenomenon whereby the rights of Blacks are acknowledged and guarded only if White lawmakers believe their decisions will benefit their own desires. He outlined two rules of interest convergence:

1. The interest of blacks in achieving racial equality will be accommodated only when that interest converges with the interest of whites in policy-making positions. This convergence is far more important for gaining relief than the degree of harm suffered by blacks or the character of proof offered to prove that harm.
2. Even when interest-convergence results in an effective racial remedy, that remedy will be abrogated at the point that policymakers fear the remedial policy is threatening the superior societal status of whites, particularly those in the middle and upper classes. (p. 69)

As such, Bell contends the *Brown* decision was not a manifestation of the nation's desire to provide equal educational opportunities for Black students, but rather America's pressing need to counter Communist propaganda and critiques that "had long used stories of racial discrimination and injustice to discredit American capitalism and democracy in the eyes of the world" (Woodward, 1955, p. 131). According to Woodward, "This issue gained tremendously in poignancy when the two powers faced each other in an ideological struggle for world leadership" (p. 131). Given the amalgamation of interracial conflict at home and international conflict abroad, Franklin and Moss (1988) underscore the significance of the *Brown* decision both domestically and on the world stage: "Perhaps no public question in the United States in the twentieth century aroused more interest at home and abroad than the debate about the constitutionality of segregated public schools" (p. 366).

On the home front, since the goals of integration required White acceptance and legitimacy, resistance to integration, as demonstrated by the Black Power movement of the 1960s, did not have "the persuasive power of the Civil Rights movement with its appeal to the moral conscience of America" (Walters, 2008, p. 108). Because the Civil Rights movement employed "normal institutional methods of social change" and had "tentative successes at integrating individuals into various aspects of American life," it reflected both a movement and ideology that eventually would gain the social and political support needed for legal change (p. 108), while preventing meaningful social change.

Rhetoric and Resistance

Despite the Court's unanimous support for school desegregation giv-en their ruling in *Brown I*, the decision faced massive resistance, indicating that the move toward equal education would not come without a fight. Many African Americans point to this refusal to follow *Brown* as an ex-ample of how integration was not given a chance and thus never really occurred.

Based on his experience operating a desegregation center for 17 years and working with school districts across the country on their desegrega-tion plans, Dr. Steele shared his four-dimensional framework for moving from segregation to integration and warned that "people have to stop using integration and desegregation as synonyms. There is a world of dif-ference between mixing bodies and going to a state of integration." He ex-plained that although "the laws really in essence may have been changed on the books," the practice and applications of these laws have not been realized.

> The first dimension that you have to deal with is access, and that's what *Brown* dealt with—giving people access to the schools. But then there's another step—I call that the body mixing—people just sitting by folks. . . the next step is looking at the process, looking at the corporate culture of the institu-tion. Also . . . you look at the micro notion of access rather than just going to the building and stuff, but look at the classes, look at who is in special ed, who's in advanced college placement. There's a perception that people have that, well, if you're Black then you can't learn. So you have to look at that whole process . . . look at the policies and procedures. People want to run de-segregated schools using the same policies and procedures that they used to run the segregated school.

He then outlined the fourth dimension of the model of segregation to in-tegration, which is *transfer*, more specifically, the ability to "transfer those things that will give you equal pay, privilege, and prestige."

"Desegregated institutions are where you [have] the bodies mixed. Integrated [institutions] are where there is a different corporate culture." Unfortunately, he added that once people "mix the bodies" they declare, "'Oh we've got an integrated institution.'" In sum, "you need all four of those dimensions before you can talk about a truly integrated [institu-tion]. You have a lot of desegregated institutions, but you don't have any integrated institutions." Dr. Cooper's responses echoed this sentiment.

We've never truly integrated. At best, we did . . . structural desegregation. We mixed children. . . . I think the commitment
has never been there [for] true integration. I think some states,
some school districts have handled it better than others. Having worked in [a school district in the South], I was rather impressed, rather surprisingly impressed with some of the policy
decisions that that school board made in a genuine interest to
facilitate genuine integration. They were aware that there was
the inclination for people who felt forced to go to school with
people unlike themselves [to] find ways of being in the building,
but never in the same classes.

According to Dr. Lewis, in [the city he worked in], it was not uncommon for county school districts to pay city schools "to accept their
Black youngsters so that they wouldn't have to teach them." This transfer of Black students to the city further segregated the school system,
making the district a constitutional violator. When told to integrate,
there weren't enough White kids left in the city schools to demonstrate
meaningful integration. Therefore, the state was also in violation of the
constitution and ordered to pay for the desegregation plan; however,
"in the beginning years, the federal government had to take funds out
of the treasury because the [state] legislature wouldn't appropriate the
money." Despite these extreme measures, today [the school district] is
"in my judgment . . . back where we were in, say, 1964," stated Dr.
Lewis.

Dr. Young believes this particular trend exists beyond any one particular community, as is evident in various districts and communities across
the country.

You know there's still some places in America where the court
rulings in the last, say, 20, 30 years have created integration,
and now people are saying, "Ah, but that costs too much money
and maybe the results aren't there, and we'd rather be in our
own Black schools and our own White schools" . . . just trying
to go back.

When asked about his thoughts concerning his local school district's
move to return to the neighborhood school pattern, which is based on
segregated housing patterns, Dr. Lewis replied, "It's, you know [chuck-
ling] the powers that be. The folks that control the thing, that's the way
they want it. That's the way they want it." Such documented examples

of White resistance and institutional and individual racism illustrate the ways that the racial tension and the climate of racial intolerance have affected the experiences of Black students post-*Brown* and, quite possibly, for generations to come. In fact, the 2007 *Parents Involved in Community Schools* decision is an example of such a setback for public education.

EDUCATION AS A CIVIL RIGHT

In the same year, the National Alliance of Black School Educators (NABSE) launched its Education as a Civil Right initiative declaring education a public, fundamental, civil right. Through this initiative, NABSE advocates a nationwide "zero tolerance policy on illiteracy, dropout and failure," working "to raise awareness and mobilize the public, and especially members of the African American community, to more actively advocate for strategies that will result in improved academic achievement for African American students" (National Alliance of Black School Educators, 2010). These strategies aim to:

- Foster and develop through dialogue, workshops, political and civil action, and other appropriate means, an awareness of the consequences of educational underachievement in every corner of society;
- Initiate activities that will directly address the educational disparities and inequities faced by African American students and families, and bring about intended and measurable improvements in our public school systems; and
- Develop the talents, skills, and leadership within our communities that can use its collective expertise and knowledge to continuously monitor, review, and affect needed changes relative to the educational civil rights of the students and families in all parts of our society. To provide strategies and activities for use in school districts serving a significant population of African American students.

In similar terms, on March 9, 2010, standing at the historic Edmund Pettis Bridge in Selma, Alabama, U.S. Secretary of Education Arne Duncan declared education "the civil rights issue of our generation." He pledged to "work with schools and enforce laws to ensure that all children, no matter what their race, gender, disability or native origin, have a fair chance at a good future," claiming that "with a strict adherence to statutory and case law, we are going to make Dr. King's dream of a color-blind society a reality" (Duncan, 2010).

Sadly, Du Bois's prophesy of the 20th-century problem of the color line would live long after Dr. King and his dream.

TOO MUCH DELIBERATE, NOT ENOUGH SPEED

The underestimation of the power of racism and racial subordination undermined the victory accomplished in *Brown I*. According to Faltz and Leake (1996), "The wave of triumph that engulfed the black community in the wake of the *Brown* decision was soured by the realization that change would not occur" (p. 229). Indeed, *Brown I*'s promise of equal education and equal protection for Black children was diluted by *Brown II*'s "all deliberate speed" provision.

In fact, it was another year before *Brown II* occurred, when the Supreme Court made its initial effort to determine and outline how and when desegregation was to take place. The Court concluded that desegregation should occur with "all deliberate speed," and the ambiguity of that standard resulted in desegregation efforts being deferred in school districts across the country (Orfield & Eaton, 1996, p. xxi).

> If the intimacy of the old regime had its unhappy and painful aspects, so did that of the new order. Unlike the quality of mercy, it was strained. It was also temporary, and it was usually self-conscious. It was a product of *contrived circumstances*, and neither race had time to become fully accustomed to the change or feel natural in the relationship. (Woodward, 1955, p. 29, emphasis added)

Preemptive measures taken by state and local governments to avoid desegregation pre-*Brown*, coupled with White flight and massive resistance to Black children integrating into historically all-White schools after *Brown*, illustrate what many have described as a climate of racism and White self-interest that existed post-*Brown* (Bell, 2004; Tate, Ladson-Billings, & Grant, 1996; Wells, 1993). Various reactionary strategies were employed by Whites to circumvent attempts to integrate the public schools on individual, collective, and institutional levels. An individualized response was for Whites to simply flee impacted neighborhoods to avoid the possibility of having their children attend school with Black children, whom they perceived to be culturally and genetically inferior (Wells, 1993).

Schools Boards: Freedom-of-Choice Plans

A district court need not accept at face value the profession of a school board which has intentionally discriminated that it will cease to do so in the future.

—*Board of Education of Oklahoma City v. Dowell*, 1991

One massive-resistance tactic included southerners "convinc[ing] the nation that blacks were content living under segregation" (Bell, 2004, p. 13). School boards used their local authority to craft and implement legislation that authorized districts to close their schools and provide tuition vouchers to Whites, who could avoid attending schools with Blacks by selecting the schools of their choice (Wells, 1993). These efforts were referred to as "freedom-of-choice" plans and often are cited by supporters of traditional public education as the reason modern-day, school-choice plans do not support integration and diversity (Fuller, Elmore, & Orfield, 1996; Wells, 1993).

In April 1959, the Virginia General Assembly vacated its massive-resistance efforts and adopted a freedom-of-choice program, which was based on tuition grants. The Assembly also repealed Virginia's compulsory attendance laws, making school attendance a matter of local choice and preference (Alexander & Alexander, 2001). A similar program was enacted in 1965 in New Kent County, Virginia. Wells (1993) explains that "as a result of harassment by local whites and the tactics employed by state pupil-placement boards, by 1965 almost 94 percent of southern black students remained in all-black schools, and in several states only the slightest change had been made in the system of separate and unequal schools" (p. 66).

Three years later in *Green v. County School Board of New Kent County, Virginia* (1968), the Supreme Court determined that rather than "dismantling the dual system," the freedom-of-choice plan:

Operated simply to burden children and their parents with a responsibility that the Court had placed squarely on the School Board. The Board must be required to formulate a new plan and, in light of other courses which appear open to the Board, such as zoning, fashion steps which promise realistically to convert promptly to a system without a "white" school and a "Negro" school, but just schools.

In fact, throughout the plan's 3 years of operation, no White student elected to attend the all-Black school, and despite 115 Negro students enrolling in the formerly all-White school in 1967, 85% of the Negro students still attended the all-Black school. The system was still dual with no intention of complying with *Brown II*.

State and Local Governments: School Assignment Plans and School Closures

State and local governments also circumvented desegregation. Virginia provides one example of this in the passage of the Virginia Pupil Placement Act of 1964, through which state placement boards "required that student transfers not upset: (1) the orderly administration of the public schools, (2) the competent instruction of the pupils enrolled, or (3) the health, safety, education, and general welfare of the pupils" (Wells, 1993, p. 65). These highly subjective measures made it nearly impossible for Black students to attend the schools without violating one, if not all, of the indicated criteria. Today, this tactic correlates with concerns expressed by school choice opponents who believe unresolved issues such as transportation, capacity, and safety may be used as indirect methods to ensure schools of choice exclude students who may upset the above criteria (Fuller, Elmore, & Orfield, 1996; Wells, 2003).

In *Griffin v. County School Board of Prince Edward County* (1964), the Supreme Court determined that a Virginia law permitting the closing of all public schools in Prince Edward County was unconstitutional. In a special session, the Virginia General Assembly passed legislation that closed and cut off state funds to public schools where White and Black children were enrolled together. Further, using the money previously allocated to the closed public schools, the state provided tuition vouchers to White students who attended newly established private segregated schools, and granted state-funded retirement benefits to the teachers of these new schools (Alexander & Alexander, 2001). Tate, Ladson-Billings, and Grant (1996) concluded that educational equality under *Brown*'s definition is incapable of producing "the expansive vision of equality that will lead to equal educational outcomes regardless of physical placement of students" (p. 47). They further observed that "the major gains blacks thought were obtainable with the desegregation model were the very ones lost as a result of not accounting for an important law of the system, white self-interest" (p. 37).

CONCLUSION

The empty promise of integration and converging interests manifested themselves in a misguided rationale for school desegregation, racial rhetoric concerning equality and integration, and resistance to such noble goals. White self-interest, which governed the unwillingness of many White communities to fund or support costs associated with desegregation (while being enthusiastic about paying to keep Black children out of White schools and Black college students out of their state higher education institutions), further contributed to why the promise of *Brown* remains empty and the concerns of Du Bois remain relevant.

After decades of fighting on the front lines for racial justice, Civil Rights attorney and law professor Charles Ogletree (2004) reflected on the *Brown* decision:

> With fifty years of hindsight, I believe that the tragic lesson of the two decisions in *Brown v. Board of Education* is that one described the aspirations of America's democratic liberalism (*Brown I*) and the other (*Brown II*) actually defined the reality of grudging educational reform and the power of racism as a barrier to true racial progress in twentieth-century, and for that matter, twenty-first century America. (p. 306)

Such reluctant efforts to pursue and realize meaningful educational reform and equality are further complicated given the 21st-century discourse of colorblindness, racial transcendence, diversity, and inclusion. Rather than removing the badges of servitude and inferiority, vestiges of slavery and segregation, we find ourselves troubled by the mixed legacy of mixed schools (Horsford, 2010b) and "illusion of black progress" (Adair, 1984). Not only are we still grappling with the vestiges of segregation, but now too the *vestiges of desegregation*.

• CHAPTER 4 •

Vestiges of Desegregation: Proximity Without Affinity

> We do not have to look very far to see the pernicious effects of a desegregated society that is not integrated. It leads to "physical proximity without spiritual affinity." It gives us a society where men are physically desegregated and spiritually segregated, where elbows are together and hearts are apart. It gives us special togetherness and spiritual apartness. It leaves us with stagnant equality of sameness rather than a constructive equality of oneness.
>
> —Dr. Martin Luther King, Jr.,
> "The Ethical Demands for Integration," December 27, 1962

Since the early 1990s, the courts and federal policy have used a "vestiges" analysis in both preK–12 and higher education to determine whether the segregationist laws and practices of the past in fact have limited educational access and opportunities for African Americans. Cases such as *Oklahoma City v. Dowell* (1991) and *Freeman v. Pitts* (1991) (and *Ayers v. Fordice* in the case of higher education) sought to ensure that school districts were putting an end to their discriminatory and segregationist practices. And while, as Thurgood Marshall wrote in his dissent to *Oklahoma City v. Dowell*, "the [Supreme] Court has never explicitly defined what constitutes a 'vestige' of state-enforced segregation," the concept is critical to determining "whether the vestiges of past discrimination have been eliminated to the extent practicable."

More than 20 years earlier, in *Green v. County School Board of New Kent County* (1968), desegregation remedies were developed to ensure policies and practices of segregation were eliminated "root and branch," and a series of strategies designed to advance the short-term goal of desegregation were enacted in school districts across the country.

CONSEQUENCES FOR BLACK FAMILIES,
SCHOOLS, AND COMMUNITIES

School desegregation was an important and necessary step in eliminating the state-sanctioned segregation that limited educational access and opportunities to Black children throughout the United States. Separate schools were, in fact, never equal. It is important, however, to note the unintended, or arguably, intended, consequences (Tillman, 2004b) of desegregation that have diminished the promise of *Brown* in the eyes of many Black Americans who discovered that the law was neither neutral, meritocratic, nor colorblind. In this section, I highlight four significant consequences for Black schools, families, and communities post-desegregation: (1) the closing of Black schools, (2) loss of jobs for Black educators, (3) burden of busing and hostile conditions faced by Black children and families attending newly desegregated schools, and (4) dismantling of the Black community.

Closing of Black Schools

One strategy, employed by Whites at the individual and neighborhood levels, was simply to flee the communities where schools would be desegregated to avoid the possibility of having Black children, who were perceived to be culturally and genetically inferior, attend school with their White children (Afrik, 1993; Bell, 2004; Ladson-Billings, 2004; Wells, 1993). On an institutional level, school boards used their local authority to craft and implement legislation that authorized districts to close their schools and provide tuition vouchers or "freedom-of-choice" plans, as they were called in Virginia, to Whites, allowing them to avoid attending schools with Blacks (Alexander & Alexander, 2000; Wells, 1993). This effort left Black students in these areas with no schools to attend.

Superintendent Cooper remembered how the school districts she worked for mobilized Black teachers to travel to and educate Black students in those communities that no longer had schools.

> There were teachers in my school and in my school district who did go [to a community impacted by school closures] in the summers and worked with those Black students who had been deprived of an education. I was . . . going to summer school for graduate work and . . . was never able to go . . . but that's when I became aware of just how resistant [some White communities] were.

Not only did the closure of schools have a significant negative effect on the education of Black students, but it also had a devastating impact on the employment status of, and opportunities for, aspiring and practicing Black educators.

Loss of Jobs and Opportunities for Black Educators

One of the most disastrous long-term consequences of desegregation for American education has been "the wholesale firing of Black educators" (Tillman, 2004b). Not only did the across-the-board demotion and firing of Black teachers, principals, and (to a lesser extent) superintendents significantly impact these educators directly, but it devastated the Black community, which since the time of desegregation, had a large number of its middle-class members employed in the field of education (Fairclough, 2004; M. Foster, 1997; Tillman, 2004b; Walker, 1996, 2000, 2001). Indeed the extensive firing of Black education professionals has "threatened the economic, social, and cultural structure of the Black community, and ultimately the social, emotional, and academic success of Black children," then and now (Tillman, 2004b, p. 280). Table 4.1 summarizes the impact of desegregation on the employment of Black educators.

In 1954, Superintendent Baker was enrolled in an all-Black teachers college in the mid-Atlantic and wondered how the *Brown* decision would affect her aspirations of becoming a teacher. Although her college was well regarded nationally, and the students always believed they "could almost go anywhere, get a job, and do well," there was also a White teachers college in town, and she recalled her classmates and herself trying to determine how desegregation would impact their job prospects. "What would happen to the Black school district and the White school district? How would the Black district be treated? Who would surface at the top?" After running through the series of questions, she revealed the answer wryly, "And you know who surfaced—the Whites were in charge." In an effort to "develop some [racial] balance," the Black and White teachers colleges merged and became a desegregated institution.

Although she knew Whites were getting most of the teaching and administrative jobs that were available, she was not particularly worried. Dr. Baker said that she and her classmates "knew we were getting a first-class education so there was not a worry about how we would fare." What they did not know, at the time, was how school desegregation would limit employment options for Black educators. With a "surplus of teachers" and most jobs going to Whites, Black educators were forced to seek teaching and administrative positions outside of their local community, city, and even field of expertise.

TABLE 4.1. Impact of School Desegregation on Employment of Black Educators

Pre-1954	Approximately 82,000 Black teachers taught 2 million Black children who attended mostly segregated schools.
1954	On May 17, the U.S. Supreme Court ruled in *Brown v. Board of Education*.
1954–1965	More than 38,000 Black educators in 17 southern and border states were dismissed from their positions.
1975–1985	The number of Black students who chose teacher education as a major declined by 66%.
1984–1989	New teacher certification requirements and teacher education program admission requirements resulted in the displacement of 21,515 Black teachers. African American teachers represented 6% of the public school teaching force, whereas African American students represented 17.1% of the public school student population.

Sources. Ethridge (1979); Hudson & Holmes (1994); Orfield & Lee (2004); Tillman (2004b)

In the case of Superintendent Lewis, the Black teachers college he was attending in the late 1950s closed once the city decided to desegregate. He explained matter-of-factly:

That's the way it happens. When integration comes, whatever was Black . . . gets closed. So [the Black teachers college] was closed. Many of the professors who taught [there] had to then go back into the high schools. The president of [the college], Dr. Johnson, who was an extremely knowledgeable young lady . . .was given a central office do-nothing position and then someone with a master's degree, a [White] high school principal, was named president of [the newly desegregated teachers college].

But the implications of such decisions would have much greater impact than any of them ever imagined. For as Dr. Baker explained:

Frankly, there is a decline in the number of African Americans in administration. Decline in the number in the superintendency. . . . I think it's a real problem. . . . We've got to find a way to train more Black teachers. Because some of our children, particularly in urban areas or anywhere, they're not going to see a teacher that looks like them during their whole career.

Burden on Black Students and Parents

In making his case against the constitutionality of segregated schools in *Brown v. Board of Education* (1954), Civil Rights attorney and later U.S. Supreme Court Justice Thurgood Marshall emphasized the harmful nature of the "stigma of inferiority" on Black children. Irons (2002) restated Marshall's argument in his book, *Jim Crow's Children*:

> What made the enforced separation of black children from white most damaging . . . was not tattered books or untrained teachers, but the stigma of inferiority that segregation inflicted on black children. School officials could buy newer books and hire better teachers for black children, but they could not erase feelings of inferiority from their minds. (p. 63)

Whereas Justice Marshall was considering the damaging effects of segregation on the psyche of Black children, these superintendents also considered the damaging effects of desegregation on Black students. Moreover, they considered the possibility that the "stigma of inferiority" was reified within the current context of schools, whereby students often experience "de facto" segregation.

Former superintendent Marshall expressed his concern, saying ways must be found to "prevent students from becoming resegregated in a desegregated environment." For him, that possibility "was worse than being segregated." He continued:

> Within the segregated environment, it seems that there [was]
> a bit more nurturing going on . . . more ways where students
> would be inspired to achieve, rather than being relegated to
> some back room, or down in the basement, or becoming an
> untouchable within that environment with low expectations.
> And when people have low expectations, they blame the victim
> rather than assume responsibility for their learning.

The irony here is that the basis of the case for school desegregation as put forth in *Brown* was the notion that separate schools for Black and White children psychologically damaged the self-concept of Black children by stigmatizing them as inferior in the eyes of the law. However, low expectations and resistance to fulfilling the spirit behind desegregation may, as many of the superintendents feared, be re-creating segregated schooling and "the stigma of inferiority" that Justice Marshall hoped the *Brown* decision would eradicate.

In fact, some wondered whether the desegregation of schools is even more destructive than segregation. Dr. Wells recalled how the newly desegregated school environment experienced by her younger siblings "was actually worse in terms of their social-emotional development." Her younger sister was the first in her family to attend a newly desegregated high school. She shared how her sister graduated a year early through extra credits and stellar academic performance:

> She had the highest grade in her class, but it was the high school principal . . . who was determined that she was not going to be the valedictorian. The valedictorian was not going to be a Black female in the first or second year of the desegregation. In the end, the principal decided that there would be no valedictorian and no salutatorians, and that there would be six honor students, and my sister would be among the six. But the ones who were chosen to deliver the addresses—the student addresses . . . were two Whites, not my sister.

According to Dr. Wells, this experience had a devastating impact on her sister's attitude toward White people and her conceptions of meritocracy.

> [The school administration] waited until all of my siblings had graduated from that particular school before they reinstituted salutatorian and valedictorian. . . . It was a small school . . . they thought we were the only, I guess, challenge to the White establishment . . . so my sister harbored that sort of resentment, the bitterness, and we all remember it very vividly that she was denied that opportunity simply because she was Black. There was no other reason.

Dismantling of the Black Community

The dismantling of the *communal bonds* (Morris, 1999, 2009) and support enjoyed by Black students, families, and educators in segregated contexts is considered a negative consequence of desegregation (Dempsey & Noblit, 1993; Horsford, 2009a; Horsford & McKenzie, 2008; Lightfoot,

1980; Morris, 2008). In his case study of a predominately Black school in St. Louis, Missouri, Morris (1999) described how the school created and sustained meaningful relations with its local African American families despite the seemingly "fragile connection" between and among many Black schools, families, and communities in the post-*Brown* era (p. 585). Contemporary social, political, and economic conditions that exist despite or because of the "gains" of the Civil Rights movement have ushered in the era of "school resegregation" or what Orfield (2005) described as a "backward slide toward renewed segregation" (p. 2).

These conditions also reveal how the *Brown* decision and subsequent desegregation policies not only dismantled government-sanctioned segregation in schools, but arguably dismantled the strong sense of community enjoyed by many African Americans prior to *Brown*, while revealing more complex and insidious manifestations of structural racism in contemporary contexts. Walters (2008) contends that integration's emphasis "on upward mobility for the Black middle class . . . resulted in the loss of autonomous power through the weakening of the collective Black community's resource structures" and "social disorganization of the Black community" (p. 109).

DIVERSITY AS EDUCATION POLICY: THE ILLUSION OF INCLUSION

> Why would a Black mother proudly tell her neighbor that her eight year old daughter performed in a ballet in her integrated school by playing her role while in a trash can on the stage?
> — Adair, *Desegregation: The Illusion of Black Progress*, 1984

In addition to bearing the burden of transforming racially isolated schools and systems into integrated institutions through busing, or attending school or work in distant communities, Black families and educators were forced to face individual and institutional acts of racism and resistance to integration in various forms. These included the sifting and sorting of students by race, as well as the false provision of equal educational access, opportunities, and resources due to the lack of support for meaningful integration.

Although it is impossible to essentialize the expectations of Black Americans concerning the *Brown* decision, these superintendents articulated hopes that school desegregation would provide equal educational access, opportunities, and resources to Black children who were disenfranchised under a racially segregated dual and unequal education system. Former Superintendent Steele said Black people believed the *Brown* decision "was going to be the hope and the change—from unequal segregation and from unequal opportunities and resources." However, he believed that, in general, people were mistaken in their understanding of what Black people were hoping to realize through the abolishment of Jim Crow.

> People thought the Black folks were bringing the suit so they could sit by White kids. That wasn't it. It was to equalize the resources. To make sure that Black kids' school year didn't go around the planting and harvesting season of sugar cane or cotton. Where White kids had 9 months of school, Black kids had 6 or 7 months of school. . . . But people had the notion that people were suing so they could sit by White folks, cause if they sat by White folks, they could learn.

The intent of *Brown*, according to Dr. Steele, was to get equal opportunities and resources, not merely to get to sit next to White folks in school.

Thus, despite the Court's declaration that separate schools were inherently unequal, this aim of the *Brown* ruling was not realized. The intent, according to Dr. Marshall, was "having the right to go to school wherever you want to" and "the right to have options in your education." However, as Dr. Marshall noted, *Brown*'s lack of "teeth" compromised the law's ability to make significant change. Unfortunately, much of the change that did occur was not what these superintendents and others in the Black community envisioned. The selected superintendents argued that despite the *Brown* decision and subsequent efforts to racially integrate schools, meaningful integration never really occurred.

The focus on "diversity" as opposed to acknowledging the historical context of racism and challenging it in its present form arguably has made it even more difficult to address and ultimately combat the problems associated with race and racism in education. Dr. Steele took issue with the emphasis on "diversity":

> Now that's another term. People like to talk about diversity 'cause they don't have to talk about segregation—past segregation and discrimination. That's a very neutral, nonthreatening term. "Oh, we're committed to diversity!" Because we can do that and never talk about the fact that the institution is in the state that it's in because we had policies and procedures that kept Black folks out. They can talk about it and never talk about when Blacks couldn't get into [the local university] or any other university. But if you talk about desegregation moving to integration, then you've got to own up to all the policies and procedures that you have that made that state of segregation.

In a 2008 address to the Lewis & Clark Law School on the King Holiday entitled "After *Brown*: What Would Martin Luther King Say?" Harvard Law School Dean Martha Minow made similar mention of "the shift in predominant discussions from talk of race to talk of 'diversity.'" She noted that while

> Diversity offers the crucial inclusion of people of all races, ethnicities, and religions—as well as the inclusion of people of both genders, people with disabilities, and other notable traits of variation. Yet, as with racial justice, "diversity" as a public policy goal can obscure the contrasts among eliminating exclusions, producing inclusive environments, and forging communities of mutual and generative commitment to the rights and freedoms of each member. (pp. 603–604)

She continued,

> Simply ending exclusions does not create mixed groups of people, and mixed groups of people do not necessarily embrace the vision and practices of communities forged through relationships among people mutually committed to the dignity and rights of each, relishing the freedom and creativity diverse groups of people can express together. (p. 604)

I argue that our failure to operate within the critical space in which this distinction lies, has resulted in shifting not from segregation to desegregation to integration, but from the vestiges of slavery and segregation to the *vestiges of desegregation*.

FROM VESTIGES OF SEGREGATION
TO *VESTIGES OF DESEGREGATION*

Ironically, the factors participants perceived as variables supporting and promoting the achievement of Black children during segregation (role of parents, role of teachers, and self-concept of students) are the same variables participants believed were dismantled by desegregation. The scattering of and decrease in employment opportunities for Black teachers and administrators; overrepresentation of Black students in special education, alternative education, and high school dropout statistics; and the diminished and often damaged self-concept of Black children are just some of the "vestiges" that exist as a result of desegregation.

Sifting, Sorting, and Tracking

Raising another issue in the sifting and sorting of students through ability tracking and aptitude tests, Dr. Marshall said, "I don't know of anyone that can judge the ability of another person, and I've been in this a long time." He continued, "I don't think that there is any pure evidence that tracking is any good . . . I just don't think it's worth a damn. But people tend to do it to sort [students], rather than to have a school where the whole philosophy is centered around [the belief that] if you work hard you will achieve."

In addressing this practice of sorting or tracking students according to perceived ability, which in many instances is closely connected to race (Artiles, Trent, & Palmer, 2004; Mickelson, 2001; Oakes, 1986; Oakes, Wells, Jones, & Datnow, 1997), Dr. Wells emphasized the importance of challenging these subtle and sometimes subconscious acts of racism and discrimination that create barriers for Black children. She suggested that "if people aren't vigilant about [these acts], if you're not questioning them, if you're not looking at the nuances behind those decisions, you get total resegregation within these so-called integrated classrooms many years after segregation should have ended."

Acknowledging the various contexts that developed and sustained, in the words of Superintendent Steele, the "policies and procedures" that originally "made that state of segregation," is important to understanding the current state of Black education. While reflecting on desegregation plans today, Dr. Baker remembered the time she was tasked to "see if desegregation was working" in a large southern city and "if there were still vestiges! Vestiges! And yes, there were still vestiges of discrimination." She explained the nature of many of these "vestiges":

They built the schools in the White community more elaborately than the ones in the Black community. Now they would say, we went to the [Black] community for them to tell us what they wanted, but those Black people over there didn't know the whole range of things they could have. . . . And then the Whites knew what was available or what schools should look like. And then, on the other hand, there's some Blacks who believed that we just shouldn't have the best, you know, that we can make do. So it's not a clear picture. Then, there [are] still too many Blacks who are suspended for discipline infractions. There's still too many poor teachers put in majority-Black schools. The vestiges are still there, my dear.

Special Education Placements

Whereas the labeling of Black students as "special education" or "discipline problems" often leads to these students being instructed in a setting outside the mainstream school environment, either in another classroom within the school or in a setting in another school location, this is not the only way in which Black students experience within-school segregation. Some students experience isolation within their own class-room settings. Dr. Wells shared her observations of this practice in the predominately White, affluent school district in which she was the super-intendent, noting:

> I'd walk through their classes and I would see things that were very disturbing to me: the White kids on the rug reading stories and doing animation and discussing, and the Black kids back in the back of the room with an adult tutor going over phonics. And I said to a principal one day, "What do you see wrong with this situation, this story, and what we see in this class?" And the principal couldn't see it. And I said, "There are three Black kids in this class. Where are they? Look at them and look at—and one little boy [possibly in timeout for discipline reasons]." I guess he had been misbehaving. They're images that stick with you because you know they're so wrong, and this was one of them.

While serving as superintendent of a large northeastern city district, Dr. Cooper was charged with enacting the court-ordered desegregation plan and remembered feeling "there was something somewhat faulty about the evaluation process that was used to classify students as *special ed.*" She recognized that "[many Black students] performed poorly, but not because of any physical or mental disability, but just because they hadn't always been taught." Thus, the lack of access to quality instruc-tion and educational support contributed to the large numbers of Black students identified as special education students. Dr. Clark shared this skepticism regarding the disproportionate number of children in special education today.

> I don't believe all of them belong there . . . it's a pathway to trouble as far as I'm concerned . . . I am not against special edu-cation for those who truly have that need and certainly would benefit from those resources. But I think [Black students'] par-ents don't always understand what it means to have this desig-nation.

Cultural Mismatch and Incongruence

One of the results—in fact, purposes—of desegregation was to create racially diverse educational environments for students. This change, however, also had important implications for teachers, many of whom would now represent a racial, ethnic, and/or cultural background different than her or his student. No longer could one assume that a child's classroom teacher would share the racial identity, ethnic background, and/or cultural values of her or his students, making it increasingly important for teachers to understand the students they serve, their families, and the communities from which they come. And while greater racial diversity—this important goal of desegregation—certainly has its social and educational benefits, many researchers have observed how *cultural mismatch* or incongruence (where students experience incompatibility between home and school) have introduced new challenges for today's teachers and principals (Boykin, 1986; Gay, 2000, 2002; Hale-Benson, 1986; Hilliard, 1967; Irvine, 1991; Ladson-Billings, 1994; Pollard & Ajirotutu, 2000). The research literature has reflects how such cultural mismatch can lead to *cultural conflict* (Delpit, 2001), *cultural collision* (Beachum & McCray, 2004, 2008), and in more troubling scenarios, *cultural collusion,* where teachers and school leaders implicitly usher out those students whose culture is not welcomed or valued in the classroom or school (Beachum & McCray, 2004).

Arguably, these realities place an even greater responsibility upon the school leader for ensuring socially just and equitable learning environments for their increasingly diverse school communities (Brooks & Miles, 2010; Dancy & Horsford, 2010; Dantley & Tillman, 2006; Marshall & Oliva, 2010; Rusch & Horsford, 2009; Skrla, McKenzie, & Scheurich, 2008; Scheurich & Young, 1997; Tillman, 2002). These challenges, however, are not insurmountable. They simply require careful attention to the philosophies, perspectives, and practices of teachers as influenced by the school and organizational culture established by their school leaders. In schools and school systems where teachers and leaders are not willing (due to deficit thinking or preconceived notions about certain students or families) or able (through limited training and preparation) to meet the distinct needs of their diverse student populations, the possibility of equal education is limited and purpose of quality public education is lost.

School–Family–Community Disconnects

Interdependence between the African American school, family, and community was the cornerstone of successful educational success enjoyed by Black students pre-*Brown* (Morris, 2009; Tillman, 2004b). As discussed in Chapter 2, Walker's (2000) consistent characteristics of Black schools under segregation included exemplary teachers, rich curriculum and extracurricular offerings, parental support, and strong principal leadership. In stark contrast, contemporary schooling environments, particularly urban settings with high concentrations of poor and African American student populations, are criticized for suffering from a lack of qualified and caring teachers, unchallenging and limited curricular and extracurricular opportunities, a lack or absence of parental involvement, and school principals who are not connected to their communities.

Indeed, the future of equal education and the successful education of Black students require a serious look at locating children at the center of our efforts to forge and foster meaningful school–home connections with African American families. They also require an assessment of the power relationships that exist between low-income and historically disenfranchised communities and the schools that serve them. As Sarah Lawrence Lightfoot (1980) noted in her chapter entitled "Families as Educators: The Forgotten People of *Brown*," it is critical that efforts to equalize the educational opportunities and experiences of Black children consider the role of parents in not only schooling, but the much broader project of education.

UNDERESTIMATING THE PREJUDICE OF RACE

There are many reasons why, as Dr. Cooper put it, "we've never truly integrated." Some scholars believe the promise of *Brown* was not realized because it overlooked the existence of race as a social construct (Bell, 2004; Ladson-Billings & Tate, 1995). Others contend the promise of integration and racial equality should not be abandoned, but rather pursued in the same spirit as *Brown* to combat the current trend toward resegregation and racial isolation (Kozol, 2005; Orfield & Eaton, 1996; Wells, 1993).

Many of the African Americans who fought vigorously against Jim Crow and for racial integration believed that once the laws changed, equal access, resources, and opportunities would follow, and the *Brown* decision was the promise of change to come. And friends of the movement, Whites and other non-Blacks, were just as committed in their efforts to dismantle the cruel system of apartheid in U.S. schools. While this exemplar of cross-racial unity and mutual respect exemplified the types of relationships and interaction advocates for integration were fighting for, those shared experiences during the struggle for Civil Rights appear to have come to a point of departure roughly 57 years later.

While all parties involved and observers alike acknowledge the limitations of *Brown* and school desegregation across the United States, the reflections and subsequent opinions of individuals regarding the continued promotion of desegregation and race-conscious education policies appear to divide along the color line. Even in the corpus of scholarship concerning school desegregation and integration, we see two contrasting perspectives that are strongly correlated to the racial identity of the individuals holding the opinion.

For example, although Orfield & Eaton (1996) argued that "the memory of good Black schools is not entirely inaccurate, but . . . obscures the substantial educational gains of Blacks in the desegregation era" (p. 84), it is important to interrogate whether these perceived gains outweigh the costs suffered by Black students, families, and communities, as presented in this chapter. In fact, my research findings, like many others, disrupt Orfield's perception of "substantial educational gains" in light of the subsequent closure of Black schools, loss of Black educators, and overrepresentation of Black students in low-ability tracks, special education programs, and behavioral schools. Ironically, the very sense of inferiority and diminished self-concept among Black students that the *Brown* decision sought to remedy, are significant considerations that must be part of any discussion concerning the possible benefits of desegregation.

White scholars not only possess a racial standpoint that is different from those of the superintendents featured here, but they enjoy the privilege of being able to speak about the virtues of school desegregation without having lived through some of the challenges and negative consequences associated with school desegregation as experienced by Black students, educators, and communities. As Ladson-Billings and Tate (1995) noted in their pivotal work that introduced critical race theory to the field of education, the "savage inequalities" that Kozol graphically illustrated in his 1991 book of the same name "are a logical and predictable result of a racialized society in which discussions of race and racism continue to be muted and marginalized" (p. 47).

This commentary not only sheds further light on the salience of racism in education, but also demonstrates how varying racial standpoints play a critical role in how individuals interpret the role of race and racism in education. As Jackson (2008) concluded, "Most of the scholars and lawyers who commented on *Brown* after 50 years agreed that *Brown I* (1954) reinforced the American Creed . . . but that *Brown II* (1955) faced the reality that racism and White supremacy were still dominant throughout the country" (p. 140).

CONCLUSION

The education of African American children suffered from a new set of problems post-desegregation (Horsford, 2010b; Horsford & McKenzie, 2008). The closing of Black schools, disproportionate burden on Black students and families, and dismantling of the communal bonds that supported schools, families, and neighborhoods influenced the education of Black children in important ways. Ironically, much of the discourse concerning school desegregation has failed to account for the salience of racism that served as the catalyst for the manifestation of racial segregation in all areas of American life, including schools. While some have argued that desegregation efforts that do not result in integration may seem like a step back to "separate-but-equal," Bell (1995) observed that "some Black educators, however, see major educational benefits in schools where Black children, parents, and teachers can utilize the real cultural strengths of the Black community to overcome the many barriers to educational achievement" (p. 26).

In my interview with Superintendent Clark, she wanted to be certain that her critique of desegregation efforts would not be used as an excuse to not continue the pursuit of meaningful integration. She succeeded educationally and professionally as a result of her segregated schooling experience, but expressed concern for how some people's frustration with *Brown* or desegregation fatigue may take us back to a time that, despite some positive aspects, was unfair and unjust.

> I don't want us to go back to separate-but-equal because I don't
> think it was ever separate-but-equal. And although I came out
> of that kind of environment from my early education . . . I think
> there's more out there for us to push for and benefit from. . . .
> We don't have the resources to go back to separate-but-equal,
> and we would not ever get the equal. We'd be separate, but we
> wouldn't get the equal.

Her words reminded me of those published more than 75 years earlier by Du Bois (1935), acknowledging, "Other things being equal, the mixed school is the broader, more natural basis for the education of all youth" (p. 335).

"But other things seldom are equal."

• Part III •

THE
INTEGRATION
GOAL

CHAPTER 5

A Burning House:
The Disintegration of Integration

The problem of race remains America's greatest moral dilemma. . . . The
price that America must pay for the continued oppression of the Negro
is the price of its own destruction.

—Dr. Martin Luther King, Jr.,
"The Ethical Demands for Integration," 1962

Shortly before his death in 1968, and several years after many of his
speeches and writings concerning his philosophy of integration, Dr. Martin Luther King, Jr., shocked his confidants and fellow activists at a strategy meeting in New York at the home of his longtime friend, singer and
actor Harry Belafonte. He told them:

> We have fought hard and long for integration, as I believe we
> should have, and I know that we will win. But I've come to
> believe we're integrating into a burning house. . . . I'm afraid
> that America may be losing what moral vision she may have
> had. . . . And I'm afraid that even as we integrate, we are
> walking into a place that does not understand that this nation
> needs to be deeply concerned with the plight of the poor and
> disenfranchised. Until we commit ourselves to ensuring that the
> underclass is given justice and opportunity, we will continue to
> perpetuate the anger and violence that tears at the soul of this
> nation.

According to Belafonte, King was preoccupied, pensive, and had
come to the realization that the idea of integration was not going to be as
straightforward as they had hoped it would be. In her personal account
of the same meeting, Marian Wright Edelman (2008) recalled, "Dr. King
was deeply discouraged about the ability of our economic system as it

currently operated to confront the deep structural ills of the racism, excessive materialism, poverty, and militarism he warned could lead to our downfall" (pp. 102–103).

His prophetic discontent concerning issues of racism, poverty, and the war in Vietnam "meant that Blacks might be integrating into a 'burning house' that exhibited immoral values, materialism, and the neglect of poor people," rendering the primary goal of integration inadequate and insufficient (Walters, 2008, p. 109). Indeed, this realization would impact not only his disappointment with the disintegration of the integration ideal due to White resistance, but, more broadly, a lack of moral vision that would continue to plague our nation and the world (Edelman, 2008; King, 1962/1986).

DANGEROUS CONDITIONS: A LOSS OF MORAL VISION

More than 40 years after that pivotal meeting, roughly 13.3 million U.S. children live in poverty and roughly 1 in 13 lives in extreme poverty (Children's Defense Fund, 2008; National Center for Child Poverty, 2010). They do not have access to health care. They go to school and bed hungry. They are the very ones who do not enjoy the educational resources, high-quality teachers, or extracurricular offerings to which children who live in more stable, affluent communities have access—the very things that could starkly improve their life chances. In her poignant depiction of the problem of poverty affecting U.S. children, child advocate and founder of the Children's Defense Fund Marian Wright Edelman (2008) paints the picture of America's Sixth Child—likening America to a family of six children, where the sixth child lacks food, clothing, shelter, quality schools, and an overall concern for her well-being. America's Sixth Child represents the one out of every six children in America who does not enjoy life, liberty, or the pursuit of happiness because of what Edelman described as a lack of moral leadership and commitment to our nation's future. She warned:

> The U.S. has exerted and continues to wield disproportionate global influence as sole remaining "superpower." But our moral authority, economic capacity, and ability to lead will continue to wane unless we get our house in order, practice our espoused values of freedom and justice, repair our crumbling economy, and create the public education systems needed to prepare our children and country to compete in the years ahead. (p. 100)

Indeed, our systems of public education are critical to not only the social and academic growth and success of our children, but also our nation's ability to compete in an increasingly international and global society, due to what Zhao (2009) characterizes as the "death of distance." While this argument has guided national efforts to ensure the United States is more competitive on an international scale, a case made strongly in *A Nation at Risk: The Imperative for Educational Reform* (1983), and subsequently supported in the No Child Left Behind Act of 2001 and A Blueprint for Reform: The Reauthorization of the Elementary and Secondary Education Act (2010), this changing social, political, and economic landscape has huge implications for the future and demands a clear moral vision for the role that schools and education will play in this brave new world.

Strong schools support and sustain strong communities, but the relationship is bidirectional, rendering schools subject to the devastating social forces of poverty, unemployment, crime, and violence. In fact, social science researchers have argued that efforts to equalize education will never be accomplished without systemic and meaningful social change as it relates to employment, housing, and other aspects of American life (Anyon, 1997; Noguera, 2008). This lack of moral vision has created dangerous conditions for not only children living in poor and historically underserved communities, but also their peers, who may remain oblivious to the disparities in educational access, opportunities, and outcomes perpetrated and perpetuated by this void in moral vision, authority, and leadership. Although many factors contribute to these perilous conditions, the purpose of this chapter is to examine more closely the problem of unequal education by centering race and racism within the larger discourse of school desegregation, integration, and equality. Because poverty continues to correlate so heavily with race in the United States and, as Dr. King observed, "the problem of race remains America's greatest moral dilemma," this chapter brings the issue of race to the fore to illustrate how and why the field of education is still plagued by gaps, disparities, and deficiencies along the color line in predictable fashion (Horsford, 2010a).

Using critical race theory's critique of liberalism as a conceptual framework, I discuss the myth of colorblindness, the myth of the neutrality of education policy, and the myth of equal opportunity and meritocracy to demonstrate how the original goal and ideal of integration has disintegrated as a result of the "racially neutral politics" of education (López, 2003).

FANNING THE FLAMES: THE PROBLEM WITH LIBERALISM

The ideology of racial liberalism has shaped much of the discourse on school desegregation, integration, and diversity in education. In her 2004 article, "From Racial Liberalism to Racial Literacy: *Brown v. Board of Education* and the Interest-Divergence Dilemma," legal scholar Lani Guinier described racial liberalism as an ideological framework within the context of Jim Crow segregation that focused on "individual prejudice" over "intentional discrimination" and "emphasized the corrosive effect of individual prejudice and the importance of interracial contact in promoting tolerance" (p. 95).

In our attempts as a nation to transition from segregation statutes to the integration ideal, the practice of desegregating White schools with Black bodies took precedence over what would be a more appropriate definition of equality in the struggle for equal education—"the fair and just distribution of resources" (Guinier, 2004, p. 95). However, rather than interrogating race and racism (López & Parker, 2003) and the racial ideologies that supported and guided segregationist practices, we sought to treat the symptoms of racism, but never the disease. As a result, critical race scholarship remains dissatisfied with liberalism's conceptualization of America's problems of race and racism (Delgado & Stefancic, 2001).

Racial liberalism's allegiance to the ideals of race neutrality of the law (all persons treated equally under the law), colorblindness (color or race doesn't matter), and meritocracy (access and achievement are based on individual worthiness), rather than the pursuit of educational equality as the fair and just distribution of resources in schools and school systems, is problematic. According to Guinier (2004), within the context of Jim Crow segregation, the conceptualization of equality as "the absence of formal, legal barriers that separated the races" and removal of the "damaging effects of segregation on black personality development" (p. 95) served as a barrier to racial justice because it failed to address structural and institutional racism. This is an argument that I believe holds true today when such limited conceptualizations of equality are applied to education, for they do not account for the unequal or unjust meting out of educational policies, programs, or processes because of structural or institutional racism, even after legal barriers have been removed. Nor do they acknowledge the limits to White personality development and cultural consciousness that result from the maintenance of separate and unequal schools.

The dismantling of racism and meaningful social change require "aggressive, color-conscious efforts" (Delgado & Stefancic, 2001, p. 22). Liberal ideologies that fail to acknowledge and consider the social construction of race as a factor in the establishment and reproduction of inequality, particularly in education, miss an important and necessary opportunity to right such historical and contemporary injustices. Moreover, the testimonies and experiential knowledge of people of color work to dispel the myths of racial liberalism's commitment to race neutrality, colorblindness, and meritocracy.

The Myth of Race Neutrality

An important critique of liberalism as expressed by critical race theo-rists is the notion that the law is racially neutral. Bell (2004) described an example of how this "neutrality" can be deemed false when undermined by acts of racism, as demonstrated by the failure of school officials to ob-serve orders to desegregate their schools.

> In St. Louis and elsewhere, school officials used the school desegrega-tion controversy to increase their legitimacy as the proper policy-making body for public education—an accomplishment furthered by the fact that civil rights lawyers like myself did not include orders calling for the replacement of school board members in our petitions for relief, even though they and their predecessors in office were responsible for the discriminatory policies and the delaying tactics we attacked in the courts. We knew they were responsible, but felt both that they would obey court orders and that relief seeking their removal would be impos-sible to obtain. (p. 124)

Thus, despite the laws being changed—laws designed to ensure that Black children would receive access to equal schooling opportunities and re-sources—the political power enjoyed by school board members, who preferred to maintain the discriminatory and racist practices from which Black students and families were seeking relief, undermined the spirit of desegregation law. Similarly, Superintendent Lewis cited examples of this failure to observe laws that would discontinue school segregation, which included historically White county school districts paying predominately Black city school districts to accept their Black students, aided by the prac-tice of "segregated busing."

Other examples of White resistance governed by both individual and institutional racism, including preemptive measures before the passage of desegregation law and blatant defiance after its passage, as discussed in Chapter 3, symbolize the ways in which law and policy do not operate in a neutral space. Social, historical, political, and cultural contexts are criti-cally important to our understanding of how and why education policies, such as desegregation, are limited in their ability to advance meaningful racial justice. While Kenneth B. Clark had hoped that busing "would help us increase human sensitivity beyond color," the advent of segregated busing quickly revealed the limitations of changing laws and policies (Clark, 1995). It seems the nation's ability to move "beyond color" may be an unrealistic and misguided goal, despite our stated values of equality, opportunity, and rewarding individuals based not on color, but on hard work and self-created success.

The Myth of Colorblindness

Unfortunately, such desires to transcend race and move beyond color have fueled a colorblind ideology that, while seeking to focus not on the color of an individual's skin, but on the content of his or her character, effectively normalizes "Whiteness," while constructing people of color as "Other." This makes it very difficult to examine the positioning and utilization of White privilege and how it becomes regarded as the societal standard, or the norm. In his 1883 "Address to the Louisville Convention," Black abolitionist Frederick Douglass captured the disingenuous nature of ignoring race only when it benefits those who have the privilege to do so. He explained:

> Though the colored man is no longer subject to be bought and sold, he is still surrounded by an adverse sentiment which fetters all his movements. In his downward course he meets with no resistance, but his course upward is resented and resisted at every step of his progress. . . . The color line meets him everywhere, and in a measure shuts him out from all respectable and profitable trades and callings. In spite of all . . . religion and laws he is a rejected man. He is rejected by trade unions, of every trade, and refused work while he lives, and burial when he dies, and yet he is asked to forget his color, and forget that which everybody else remembers.

According to DeCuir and Dixson (2004), the colorblind discourse also has been embraced as a way "to justify ignoring and dismantling race-based policies that were designed to address societal inequity (Gotanda, 1991)," (p. 29) as we observed in 2007 with the U.S. Supreme Court *Parents Involved in Community Schools v. Seattle School District No. 1, et. al* (2007) case, which deemed race-based school assignment policies in Seattle, Washington, and Louisville, Kentucky, and thus similar plans throughout the nation, unconstitutional.

Dr. Steele recollected his brother's winning a model airplane contest in the 1940s, but being unable to reap the reward of his accomplishment because the prize was a ticket to a Whites-only movie theater. Another brother of Dr. Steele "made the highest score on the Army General Classification test of anybody inducted into the Army" through his particular camp, but was deprived of the chance to become a pilot because he "was too big." Dr. Wells remembered the devastating ordeal her sister experienced when she earned the honor of being first in her class in her newly desegregated high school but was denied the opportunity to be recognized as valedictorian, as Dr. Wells put it, "simply because she was Black. There was no other reason."

These occurrences reflect participant accounts not only as students under desegregation, but also as aspiring educators, graduate students, and school superintendents. For example, Dr. Young described his extensive job search of 100 superintendent positions with no offers until he accepted a White confidante's advice to cut his Afro and wear different clothing so he would not be so intimidating to White interviewers. Dr. Clark recalled becoming a finalist for a superintendent position, and being told that although she was the most qualified for the job, it was clear that the "community was not ready for a Black person" to fill it.

While these counterstories to the ideology of colorblindness may not appear to have huge implications for equal education, they provide examples of what Bonilla-Silva (2006) conceptualized as "colorblind racism," an ideology that "explains contemporary racial inequality as the result of nonracial dynamics." He continued, "Where Jim Crow racism explained blacks' social standing as the result of their biological and moral inferiority, color-blind racism avoids such facile arguments. Instead, whites rationalize minorities' contemporary status as the product of market dynamics, naturally occurring phenomena, and blacks' imputed cultural limitations." This brand of colorblind racism is thus supported by the ideal of meritocracy.

The Myth of Meritocracy

Indeed, the myths of colorblindness and neutrality of the law work hand in hand with the false notion of meritocracy. In his primer on CRT, Taylor (1998) explained, "By relying on merit criteria or standards, the dominant group can justify its exclusion of [Blacks] to positions of power, believing in its own neutrality" (p. 123). Thus, despite their abilities, skills, and achievements, Blacks often are not fairly recognized or rewarded because they are Black. This further limits their ability to enjoy what is rightfully owed to them, opportunities and recognition that would be observed under a true merit system. He continued, "CRT asserts that such standards are chosen, they are not inevitable, and they should be openly debated and reformed in ways that no longer benefit privileged whites alone" (p. 123). This holds true for metrics often used in education, which are depicted as objective but are highly subjective, given the process by which students are identified as special education, placed in ability tracks, or selected for gifted education.

As a result, such subjective measures influence the expectations for achievement that educators may hold for students of racially underrepresented groups, poverty, and single-family homes—thus contradicting the liberal idea of meritocracy and perpetuating racial stratification and inequality. In fact, the superintendents I interviewed were concerned that, in fact, this was the case for racially underrepresented students in desegregated schools. According to Dr. Cooper:

> As our country has become more and more diverse, I'm seeing the schools almost being used to craft a caste system, because if you are trapped into an inferior education, you're going to be trapped into a lifestyle and condition of livelihood that's going to be substandard as compared to somebody else.

These structures and hierarchies are not limited to what Dr. Steele described as school systems that successfully sort and sift children according to their perceived abilities, but also determine who gets access to educational leadership positions and the level of responsibility afforded in those positions.

Superintendents shared examples of denied benefits and opportunities in desegregated contexts, where they were limited in their ability to find jobs or enjoy the same authority their White counterparts did in similar positions, debunking racial liberalism's myths of colorblindness and meritocracy (DeCuir & Dixson, 2004; Delgado & Stefancic, 2001; Guinier, 2004). Dr. Baker said, "I think some of us thought desegregation was going to give us something that it didn't give us and . . . [yet] there were certain positions you didn't get because you weren't White." When selected as a finalist for a superintendent's position, Dr. Clark was told that while she was the most qualified candidate, the "community was not ready for a Black person" to assume the role.

Even after assuming the superintendency, some participants did not feel they enjoyed the same rights as their White counterparts. They recalled feeling restricted in their ability to share and implement their vision for fear of being prevented from doing what they wanted to do. According to Dr. Marshall, "Black superintendents, many of them . . . didn't have the same power base as White superintendents to make certain kinds of decisions," such as "the authority to hire and control their situation as some of [their] White friends [did]." Furthermore, they often were hired to lead districts that Dr. Lewis described as being in "disarray," where the "infrastructure had just disintegrated," the student population was majority-Black, and "the board was fighting among itself." And still, he added, "there are some school districts . . . you know you need not apply."

ASSESSING THE DAMAGE:
THE IMPORTANCE OF STRUCTURAL INTEGRITY

Achievement and opportunity gaps, funding disparities, and unequal resources and outcomes in education continue to underscore the complex
legacy of desegregation and the still-complicated relationships between
race, educational access, opportunity, and achievement in U.S. schools
(Horsford, 2010a, 2010b). These challenges remain not by accident, but
because they are embedded in the institutional structures, systems, policies, and practices that govern and, in turn, perpetuate inequality in our
schools and society. Accordingly, the disintegration of school integration
efforts in this country cannot be attributed solely to de facto segregation
or a lukewarm commitment to the cause of equality. The reason we see
the same problem of racial inequality in education manifesting itself generation after generation is in large part due to the historical role of race
in U.S. education, the purpose of its construction, and our continued lack
of knowledge and understanding concerning its unrelenting significance
now and for future generations.

The challenge we face is the discomfort and apprehension of policymakers, educational and business leaders, and other stakeholders in dealing with the hard questions about race and its legacy of educational inequality and injustice for an ever-increasing percentage of our nation's
children and youth. It is not enough to simply review, revisit, or reframe
the problem. In fact, we have studied and seemingly admired the problem
of unequal education for so long that we have failed to hear and heed
the call for moral and just leadership in schools, particularly as it deals
explicitly with issues of race, power, and privilege. According to Oliver
Cromwell Cox (1948) in *Caste, Class, and Race*:

> We cannot defeat race prejudice by proving that it is wrong. The
> reason for this is that race prejudice is only a symptom of a ma-
> terialistic social fact. . . . The articulate white man's ideas about
> his racial superiority are rooted deeply in the social system, and
> it can be corrected only by changing the system itself.

In similar terms, Dr. King explained in 1967, 4 years after his "I Have
a Dream" speech of 1963, that:

> White Americans must recognize that justice for black people
> cannot be achieved without radical changes in the structure of
> our society. The comfortable, entrenched, the privileged cannot

continue to tremble at the prospect of change of the status quo.
. . . This is a multi-racial nation where all groups are dependent
on each other. . . . There is no separate white path to power and
fulfillment, short of social disaster, that does not share power
with black aspirations for freedom and human dignity.

Dr. King's clarion call for "radical changes in the structure of our society" demonstrated a systemic, transformative approach to social justice,
where the privileged must in fact "share power" in order to grant justice
to the oppressed.

While many continue to attribute a colorblind ideology to Dr. King
based on his dream "that my four little children will one day live in a
nation where they will not be judged by the color of their skin, but by
the content of their character," examined more deeply and collectively,
King's works and their emphasis on societal structures and the fair distribution of power and resources reveal a much broader picture of racial
and social justice that requires more than simply not "seeing" color. It
calls for changing the ways in which we attribute meaning to the social
construction of race. It necessitates acknowledgment of a power structure
that, if not dismantled, will forever disadvantage one group and privilege
another. It demands "radical changes" that will never be realized without
moral vision, leadership, and courage.

CONCLUSION

It is hard to imagine the heaviness Dr. King felt during that strategy meeting in New York with his fellow activists and friends. He was now the
servant leader who had become the face and name of a movement that
would forever change the nature of race relations in the United States,
and largely through the cause of integration. While he was able to make
great strides for racial justice and break down barriers that many thought
were indestructible, he struggled to secure support and momentum for
his Poor People's Campaign and grieved over the "anger and violence that
tears at the soul of this nation."

But to me, perhaps the most intriguing aspect of this pivotal moment
goes beyond the profundity and weight of Dr. King's burden for the cause
of social justice and the prophetic power of his words, but rather the ex-
change that followed.

Still confused and dismayed about Dr. King's remarks about "integrating into a burning house," Belafonte asked what they should do.

Despite his visible discouragement and despondency and perhaps because of his relentless commitment to the poor and disenfranchised, Dr.
King at once replied:

> "We're just going to have to become firemen."

CHAPTER 6

On Becoming Firefighters:
Our Moral Activist Duty
to Equal Education

While my use of the "burning house" metaphor was inspired by Dr. King's concern that we were "integrating into a burning house" and his subsequent charge to "become firemen," I quickly discovered that the imagery of fire and firefighting could serve as an appropriate metaphor for combating the seen and unseen dangers of racism in education. We are fighting an intense and consuming threat to the educational success and life chances of our nation's schoolchildren, requiring us to become metaphorical firefighters as we engage in the moral activist work necessary in the 21st-century struggle for equal education.

Firefighters protect life and property. Their level of preparation for the most dangerous of conditions is critical to their success in achieving their goals of defending life, property, and the environment. Through extensive training; familiarity with the nature, intensity, and danger of fire and its deadly byproducts; and sheer determination, courage, and sense of purpose, these everyday heroes are skilled, equipped, and committed to fulfill their moral duty and service. While they must plan for the worst of circumstances, they hope and, as a result, work tirelessly for the best of possible outcomes.

In the case of Dr. King, history tells us he may have been distressed over the staunch resistance to his strategies for nonviolence and the dissension that ensued between and among Black leaders concerning the future of the Civil Rights movement (Walters, 2008). Or, because the intensity and violent nature of the resistance to integration began to show itself as possibly something equally troubling and horrifying as life under Jim Crow. But despite this heightened crisis of racial discord and explosive rhetoric and resistance spewed from White supremacists, Black militants, and a government divided, which seemed to fan the flames of racialized anger and resistance, Dr. King sought a seemingly rational solution to an overwhelmingly dangerous problem, prompting me to consider a similarly measured response to the burning house of resegregated schooling and deficit thinking.

What must be done to end the day of learning in a burning house, where we have traded the problem of segregation for continued structural racism and economic exploitation? How do we develop, establish, and sustain meaningful educational change under such conditions? Considering the simplicity of Dr. King's response "to become firemen," I extend this metaphor as I often wonder what we as educators should do to put out the flames of a burning house—or the moral decay and ethical despondency that still pervade schools and schooling 5 decades after their separateness was deemed by the Court as inherently unequal.

A MORAL VISION OF EQUAL EDUCATION

The history of exclusion and discrimination in U.S. education should prepare us for the realities of race and racism as central and permanent aspects of U.S. society and schooling. While sociologist Kenneth B. Clark reluctantly acknowledged his underestimation of the embedded nature of highly resistant racism in America, he explained in his *Dark Ghetto: Dilemmas of Social Power* (1965), that "the truth of the dark ghetto is not merely a truth about Negroes; it reflects the deeper torment and anguish of the total human predicament."

Indeed, this human predicament is complex. It is uncomfortable. It is why we want to avoid, ignore, or move beyond race. As a nation, we are both haunted by and obsessed with its meaning. Yet, it is the place we continue to stand, more than 2 centuries after the founding of this nation by a document "stained with the original sin of slavery." In 2008, while the Democratic presidential nominee, Senator Barack Obama spoke directly about our nation's racial paradox, in his now famous "race" speech.

> This is where we are right now. It's a racial stalemate we've been stuck in for years. Contrary to the claims of some of my critics, Black and White, I have never been so naïve as to believe that we can get beyond our racial divisions in a single election cycle, or with a single candidacy—particularly a candidacy as imperfect as my own. . . . But I have asserted a firm conviction—a conviction rooted in my faith in God and my faith in the American people—that working together we can move beyond some of our old racial wounds, and that in fact we have no choice if we are to continue on the path of a more perfect union.

What does this "working together" look like? How do we move beyond these "racial wounds"? What are the consequences of not choosing "the path of a more perfect union"? More specifically, how do we explore and grapple with these questions in the field of education, which arguably holds the greatest potential for hope or harm.

It starts with a vision—a moral vision of equal education and the moral activism that the fulfillment of such a vision demands. Although the problem of race has social, economic, political, and legal dimensions, it remains our nation's moral dilemma (King, 1962/1986) insofar as it perpetuates inequality, discrimination, and injustice. A vision of equal education requires a solution that targets racism and racial injustice in ways that satisfy the constitutional guarantee of equal protection under the law. As Dr. King concluded a year before his death in 1968, "We must come to see that the roots of racism are very deep in our country, and there must be something positive and massive in order to get rid of all the effects of racism and the tragedies of racial injustice."

Drawing from the interdisciplinary scholarship on the construction and evolution of race and racism, particularly their roles in schooling and education, I put forth a critical race approach for equal education, heavily informed by Bonilla-Silva's (2006) conception of *colorblind racism,* Lani Guinier's (2004) theory of *racial literacy,* Derrick Bell's work on *racial realism,* and Walters's (2008) work on *racial reconciliation.* I also draw heavily from the substantive critical race theory in education research, which has made important contributions to the study of race in education (Alemán, 2007; Bell, 2004; DeCuir & Dixson, 2004; Dixson & Rousseau, 2005; Horsford, 2010a, 2010b; Ladson-Billings, 1998, 2005; Ladson-Billings & Tate, 1995; López, 2003; López & Parker, 2003; Lynn & Parker, 2006; Parker, Deyhle, & Villenas, 1999; Parker & Villalpondo, 2007; Solórzano & Yosso, 2002; Tate, 1997).

A CRITICAL RACE APPROACH TO EQUAL EDUCATION

Ironically, the quest for post-racialism, or moving beyond the historical, legal, social, and political implications of race, remains evident in those fields of study seemingly obsessed with data collected, disaggregated, correlated, analyzed, and reported according to "race," however loosely or ill defined. As one such field, educational leadership continues to measure the success of its leaders, schools, districts, and policies based on how students and schools perform by race or indicators that frequently correspond to race (i.e., ethnicity, language, special education, and socioeconomic status), while seeking to diminish the role of race as it pertains to power, privilege, social stratification, and cultural reproduction in separate and unequal schooling contexts.

The lack of understanding concerning the social construction of race and its correlation to separate and unequal schooling contexts undermines efforts to improve academic achievement for all students. It also underscores the need for educational leaders to engage in practical strategies that directly address the intractable gaps and disparities that continue to plague our schools and school systems along the color line. As such, I propose a critical race approach to equal education—a multistep progression of racial consciousness and praxis that includes the following: (1) racial literacy, (2) racial realism, (3) racial reconstruction, and (4) racial reconciliation.

Racial literacy is the ability to understand what race is, why it is, and how it is used to reproduce inequality and oppression. *Racial realism* is drawn from critical race theory's focus on acknowledging the history, pervasiveness, and salience of race and racism in U.S. society, including its schools, and the pitfalls associated with liberal education ideology, policy, and practices. *Racial reconstruction* is the process of ascribing new meaning to race in order to transform the ways we think about and, subsequently, act on our racial assumptions, attitudes, and biases, in an effort to dismantle the racial contradiction that has plagued our nation since the Constitutional Convention of 1787. And finally, *racial reconciliation* is where we seek to heal the soul wounds and damage that have been done in schools and society relating to race and racism. Table 6.1 summarizes these four steps.

Racial Literacy: Understanding What Race Is and How It Works

Race is not biological. It has no genetic basis. It is a modern idea created for a very specific purpose in the United States—to relegate a certain group of people with shared physical characteristics to a system of chattel slavery that had never before been seen in our world's history. This categorization was required to justify the economic system fueled by slavery and it denied the rights of some people to possess the freedoms enjoyed by others. This socially constructed concept of race made "natural" the notion of inequality and stratification of individuals based on their racial classification, only to be codified in U.S. law and institutionalized throughout the nation's policies, government agencies, schools, and society.

These facts concerning race are the first steps toward *racial literacy*—understanding what race is and how it works. Guinier (2004) defined racial literacy as a framework that "requires us to rethink race as an instrument of social, geographic, and economic control of both whites and

TABLE 6.1. Critical Race Approach to Equal Education

Racial Literacy	Ability to understand what race is, why it is, and how it is used to reproduce inequality and oppression
Racial Realism	Drawn from critical race theory's focus on acknowledging the history, pervasiveness, and salience of race and racism in U.S. society, including its schools, and the pitfalls associated with liberal education ideology, policy, and practices
Racial Reconstruction	The process of ascribing new meaning to race in order to transform the ways we think about and, subsequently, act on our racial assumptions, attitudes, and biases
Racial Reconciliation	Process that seeks to heal the soul wounds and damage that has been done in schools and society relating to race and racism

blacks" (p. 114) and "flexible enough to apply to different contexts without forcing everyone's experiences into a single explanatory narrative" (Guinier & Torres, 2002, p. 31). The work of Omi and Winant (1986) provides an important foundation on which to build concerning racial formation as a way to study what race is and how it operates in society. According to these authors, racial formation is the "process by which social, economic, and political forces determine the content and importance of racial categories, and by which they are in turn shaped by racial meanings" (p. 61). As such, race is "an ideological process" based on historical events and realities, and affects all aspects of social life (Omi & Winant, 1986, p. 64; see also Bonilla-Silva, 2006). Thus, when we understand that racial categories are social constructions whereby we intentionally have attached and ascribed particular meanings at the individual and institutional levels, we can effectively begin to unpack what race is, what it means, and the ways in which it successfully serves as a tool of inequality and unfair treatment and practices.

Racial Literacy in Education: Fire Prevention

Most Americans are shocked to discover that the concept of race is just an illusion (Adelman, 2003). That race is not real. That race is not biological, has no genetic basis, and that in fact, skin color is only skin deep. That race and freedom were born together, created to establish White superiority, justify social inequalities as natural, and support policies like slavery, the extermination of American Indians, the exclusion of Asian immigrants, the taking of Mexican lands, and the institutionalization of racist practices within American government, laws, and society. When we begin to understand the true purpose and function of race, and that it is not the color of one's skin, the shape of one's eye, or the texture of one's hair, but rather an idea that was created to advantage some people and disadvantage others, we are no longer surprised by gaps and disparities by race. Rather, we expect them. And *this* is when race and racism become *very* real. When we look at race as a social construction—a modern idea used to maintain a power balance that favors members of the dominant group—it is both troubling and overwhelming. How do we begin to eliminate these racial disparities, which have been perpetuated for so long and so successfully?

When we understand that the concept of race was developed to explain social inequalities and, in turn, justify discrimination, we are no longer surprised by Black–White achievement gaps, the disproportionate number of Black and Latino males in special education, or the underrepresentation of students of color in gifted or advanced placement classes. As Superintendent Steele explained, the American public school system is very successful at accomplishing what it was designed to do—sift and sort children according to race.

To be effective advocates for equal education, educators and educational leaders must be racially literate—understanding how race functions in the teaching, learning, administration, and implementation of policy at the school and school district levels. The *Brown* decision serves as just one example of how education law and policies are limited by the embedded nature of race, structural racism, and the distribution of power and resources along racial lines.

Just as firefighters must be well trained and knowledgeable of the devastating force of fire *before* ever arriving at the scene, educational leaders must be well versed in what race is, how it came to be, and how it functions in schools and society. Understanding the dynamic interplay of race, power, and privilege, and how race is socially funded (Ladson-Billings, 2010) throughout every aspect of American life, is an important construct for educators to comprehend on more than a superficial level. This is particularly important given the salient role of race as it relates to school achievement data, which are notoriously disaggregated by race, as well as income, language, and ability. Through racial literacy and a heightened awareness of how race manifests itself in many aspects of schooling, educational leaders will be better positioned to prevent or limit the devastating effects of race and racism, much as firefighters do through their fire inspections, training, and fire prevention campaigns.

In practical terms, educational leaders must not only be willing, as Beveraly Daniel Tatum (2007) suggested, to "talk about race," but also to

(1) reframe discussions of race and racism from individual attitudes and acts of prejudice and discrimination toward an examination of the structural, institutional, and administrative policies, processes, and practices that maintain and reproduce inequities in schools and school systems, and (2) think critically about the ideologies of colorblindness, integration, diversity, and inclusion that are presented in racially neutral or ahistorical ways (Horsford, 2009b). Support for diversity and inclusion programs and initiatives that fail to recognize how race and racism work to maintain hierarchies, allocate resources, and distribute power will not do much to address gaps in student achievement, low school performance, and distrusting school communities.

Racial Realism: Acknowledging Race and Racism in U.S. Society

While most people would not contest the claim that sexism is an aspect of American life, and that homosexuals and individuals with disabilities are discriminated against (although some people believe this discrimination is justifiable), the suggestion that racism still exists and is a very real problem in the 21st century continues to cause defensiveness, denunciation, and heated resistance from apologists of colorblindness. *Racial realism* is drawn from critical race theory's focus on acknowledging the history, pervasiveness, and salience of race and racism in U.S. society, including its schools, and the pitfalls associated with liberal education ideology, policy, and practices.

One of the most obvious ways to begin to acknowledge race and racism is by studying the history of discrimination and legacy of separate and unequal education in U.S. schools. There is no doubt that many want to move beyond what is a painful and unjust history documenting the mistreatment, exclusion, and segregation of schoolchildren in the United States based on racial and ethnic background, as evidenced in Texas by the controversial debate on the content in school textbooks. What parts of U.S. history should be included? What aspects should be eliminated? Who gets to decide? As they say, the winners get to write the history, and thus there are always equally important perspectives that remain untold. We can uncover these by researching not only the nation's history of education, but also the local histories of the school communities that school leaders and educators serve.

This information can be gained through historical research and artifacts, including newspaper reports, governmental data, school and district performance reports, and informal interviews that capture the experiential knowledge of people who have been marginalized, underserved, or silenced in a particular community. Similarly, encouraging practicing and aspiring educational leaders to study the historical, political, economic, and social contexts of the school communities they serve or intend to serve, fosters a racial realist perspective. Through informal interviews that capture the experiential knowledge of people who have been marginalized, underserved, or silenced in a particular community, or a review of educational policies, such as the development and implementation of a local district's desegregation plan, can offer important insight concerning how race was funded and/or functioned in a particular school community. For example, Jerome Morris's (2009) ethnographic studies of the education of Black students in urban centers such as Atlanta and St. Louis chart the migration, housing patterns, and subsequent racial desegregation and resegregation that took place as a result.

Racial Realism in Education: First Responders

Educational leaders must recognize and examine the structural and institutional manifestations of exclusion and segregation that permeate administrative structures, policies, processes, and practices, and maintain racialized hierarchies and inequities in schools and school systems. While some educators may wish to avoid such investigations, a critical race analysis of these factors is crucial to establishing a school structure and fostering a school climate and culture that support school–family–community relationships built on the mutual respect, caring, and trust that many communities of color long for today. It is important to build on both the literature documenting the history of African American education and valued segregated schools, and the negative long-term implications of desegregation for Black students, families, and communities, in order to challenge the contemporary narrative, which is void of historical context and acknowledgment of the racialized hierarchies that continue to exist in school systems, structures, and processes. These social, institutional, and community forces work together to create a contemporary schooling context for Black students that is more complex to navigate and understand.

It is also important to learn from the experiences, voices, and stories of those who came before us and have wisdom of practice and experiential knowledge. The use of counternarratives and voices of color in educational leadership courses and programs can create new opportunities to facilitate and foster discussions of race, culture, and politics in education. Several of the findings in this study provide great examples of how counterstorytelling, grounded in the experiences of people of color, may prove to be a powerful tool used to promote and provoke reaction, response, and reflections that can lead to different ways of understanding and meaning making. These accounts can provide future educational leaders with insight that will better prepare them to work with students and communities of color.

The use of such counternarratives can be shared within the context of broader race-based methodologies, which "arise because existing theoretical models and methodological discussions are insufficient to explain the complexity of racialized histories, lives, and communities" (Pillow, 2003, p. 186). Exposing aspiring educational leaders to alternative ways of living, knowing, and understanding, as uniquely experienced by individuals who are similarly raced or racialized, better prepares these students to lead in diverse schools and communities. Perhaps laying bare the narrative of White privilege, coupled with exposure to counternarratives and race-based methodologies, will prepare future educational leaders to acknowledge and embrace this fundamental responsibility.

Racial Reconstruction: Creating New Conceptions of Race

According to Foner and Mahoney (1990), in the aftermath of the Civil War, "Central to the national debate over Reconstruction was the effort by Southern blacks to breathe full meaning into their newly acquired freedom. "Blacks seized the opportunity . . . to consolidate their families and communities, establish a network of churches and other autonomous institutions, stake a claim to equal citizenship, and carve out as much independence as possible in their working lives" (p. 137).

In the post–Civil Rights era, we continue to find ourselves grappling with this seemingly intractable problem of racial injustice, requiring a new form of *racial reconstruction*—the process of ascribing new meaning to race in order to transform the ways we think about and, subsequently, act on our racial assumptions, attitudes, and biases. Similar to the first and second reconstructions that took place in the United States, we must embark on a third reconstruction in an effort to dismantle the racial contradiction that has plagued our nation since the Constitutional Convention of 1787. Since race is a social construction, an "illusion" if you will, that enjoys power primarily through the meaning that is ascribed to it, race is to some degree dynamic and malleable, given the variance in racial categories and how individuals fit into these categories over time.

But before "reconstructing" race, it is imperative that we understand the contexts and constructs that have led to the current construction of race and the current meanings ascribed to race. An ahistorical approach to racial reconstruction is, by definition, impossible, given the need to know what already exists before consciously changing it.

Racial Reconstruction in Education: Protecting Life and Property

Assumptions of Black inferiority must be acknowledged as part of the reason our nation's public schools and school systems are still not integrated today. Although many scholars continue to argue and advocate for race-conscious education policies designed to promote integration, the value of these strategies, when they are forced, contrived, and resisted by those who do not want their children to attend school with "other people's children," renders the cause of school integration empty. The findings presented in this research demonstrate the emphasis the former superintendents placed on the social context of education, including families, community members, policymakers, and social forces that greatly inform the quality of schooling Black students receive. Increased socioeconomic segregation, shifting demographics, cultural mismatch, stereotype threat, and critical race disconnects between schools and communities further complicate these contemporary contexts and call for community building that establishes a collective vision for education that seeks to restore what was lost through desegregation.

The findings also add to a larger narrative that underscores the concepts of communal bonds, interpersonal and institutional caring, and collective responsibility as important to the schooling and education of Black students in segregated contexts. It also fuels the subsequent desire of study superintendents to restore these valued aspects of segregated schools in ways that support and nurture student success in contemporary desegregated and resegregated settings. The critique of American racism in education speaks to deeply embedded structures and processes that lead to inequality through social and economic conditions that manifest themselves as disparities in access, opportunities, resources, and power. "Even when race is no longer explicitly coded by appearance or ancestry, the allocation of seats in a classroom, the use of buses to transport schoolchildren, or the hue of the dolls with which those children play, race is, and was, about the distribution of power" (Guinier, 2004, p. 99).

So long as race continues to hold predictive value concerning whether a child is located on the high or low end of "an achievement gap," is deemed "at risk" or "underserved," or remains "overrepresented" in special education or behavioral programs, or "underrepresented" in gifted or honors programs, we must work actively to reconstruct race in transformative ways that foster and forge the same equal expectations for all children. Indeed, by reconstructing our notions of race and the subsequent meaning we ascribe to racial categories and the individuals whom we place in those constructs, we can endeavor to protect the life and property of all citizens through dismantling the privilege and power enjoyed by the few based solely on race.

Racial Reconciliation: Toward Racial Healing and Harmony

As we consider race and racism, it is important to note the personal pain, suffering, and trauma that occur as a result of racial prejudice, discrimination, and injustice. This is particularly significant in the context of schooling, education, and the impact such disparate treatment has on children, especially when dispensed by those individuals who are responsible for ensuring their safety and security. In her 2009 article, "Emotional Abuse of Students of Color: The Hidden Inhumanity in Our Schools," McKenzie reflected on interview responses garnered from an interventionist action research study she conducted with White teachers of Black and Latino children in an urban elementary school in the United States. The goal of her original study "was to work alongside these teachers in a reflective process of examining our views about the students of color we worked with, our views of our own racial identity, and the relationship between these two perspectives" (p. 130).

McKenzie illustrated the many ways these "average to good" White teachers emotionally and psychologically abused their students of color by "criminalizing and pathologizing, disrespecting and blaming, and humiliating and excluding" (p. 133). Similar to the heartbreaking accounts offered in Jean Anyon's *Ghetto Schooling* (1997), McKenzie spoke directly to the shaming of these elementary-aged students of color and the abstract wounds of the psyche and spirit that result. She concluded:

> When I consider the incarceration statistics and reflect on my 25 years working in schools, I have to ask if these imprisoned adults were once the children I saw daily in our special education classes and lower level classes, the ones that were most often referred to me for discipline when I was a principal, the ones that dropped out before graduation. In other words, are these the ones we failed to teach and teach well? Then, when I am strong enough to face the answer, I ask—"are these the ones who were shamed and abused daily in our schools by our words and our practices and who did not have the resources to protect themselves?" (p. 141)

McKenzie's accounts reminded me of the historical trauma theory literature that is fairly recent in the field of public health, which I believe can be applied to what is happening in the field of education. In short, historical trauma theory is based on the premise that "populations historically subjected to long-term mass trauma exhibit a higher prevalence of disease even several generations after the original trauma occurred" (Sotero, 2006, p. 94). It originates with the subjugation of a population by a dominant group in four ways: (1) overwhelming physical and psychological violence, (2) segregation and/or displacement, (3) economic deprivation, and (4) cultural dispossession. Therefore, the purpose of studying historical trauma is to understand how it influences the current health status of racial and ethnic U.S. populations in order to provide new directions and insights for eliminating health disparities.

But one of the things that really struck me as I was reading about this theory of historical trauma was a discussion of a concept known as the "soul wound." Two researchers, who studied minority populations indigenous to a certain area (such as Native Americans) who were colonized by a dominant group (such as White Europeans), described the poor health of Native people who suffered from the collective effects of injustice and discrimination as a soul wound. And I would argue that soul wound is an accurate description of the traumatic physical, psychological, and emotional injury that African Americans have experienced as a result of slavery, segregation, and oppression.

But something about this phrase *soul wound* really caught my attention, as it seemed to capture the indescribable pain, suffering, and seemingly irreversible damage that could be experienced by a human being or group of people. So I looked up each word in the dictionary and read that a wound is described as "an injury to the body that typically involves laceration or breaking of a membrane and usually damage to underlying tissues." This can be caused by violence, surgery, or an accident. So what then is a wound of the *soul*?

The soul is defined as "the immaterial essence, animating principle, or actuating cause of human life," "the moral and emotional nature of human beings," "the spiritual principle embodied in human beings," "a person's total self." So arguably, when you talk about a "soul wound" you are talking about the laceration of one's being or the breaking of one's spirit. You are referring to the damage of the underlying tissues of the essence, the principle, the nature, of a person and a people. As guided by historical trauma theory, perhaps we can apply the same approach to understanding how the current educational status of these same populations can inform the ways in which we eliminate educational disparities by working to heal the soul wounds and damage caused by racism. This brings us to the final step in the critical race approach to equal education—*racial reconciliation*, which cannot be imposed, but must come from within.

CONCLUSION

Although many researchers have identified the benefits of desegregation, integration, and diversity in schools, this empirical study contributed to the underexplored narratives of segregated schooling, underexamined aspects of desegregation, and marginalized perspectives of color on the growing trend toward increasingly diverse but resegregated schooling in the United States. The goal of this book was not to support or defend school desegregation but to extend our understanding of integration ideology and desegregation policy as informed by the perspectives of Black superintendents who attended segregated schools and led desegregated districts. Their unique perspectives on the complex legacy of school desegregation revealed and reflected *mixed feelings* about mixed schools and uncertainty for what the future holds, given the moral dilemma of racial inequality in U.S. schools and society.

Educational leaders entrusted with serving children and families who represent historically excluded and segregated populations must be racially literate—understanding why separate and unequal education persists and what should and could be done about it. Failure to acknowledge such legacies of exclusion, segregation, discrimination, and injustice by race in U.S. education limits not only the effectiveness of educational leaders but also education researchers who seek to inform public policy and practice in ways that advance racial, economic, and social justice in schools. Without a racially literate understanding of why educational inequities and injustices exist in the first place, educational leaders and scholars alike will be hard pressed in their efforts to resist and transform the educational structures and systems that reproduce and maintain the unequal inputs and outcomes they seek to disrupt.

Although this study asserts, as many others have before it, that highly resistant racism, coupled with liberal integration ideology, is why the promise of *Brown* remains empty, perhaps its chief contribution lies in its call to rethink race and reframe *equality* in our work to ensure equal education for America's children. By moving from racial liberalism to racial literacy, educational leaders will better understand why school desegregation policies and strategies have not worked, why they do not guarantee equal education, and why they should serve as only one of many possible approaches to providing a rigorous, proper, and equal education for all children despite their race or life circumstances. By rethinking race as a consciously constructed tool used to control the social, economic, and geographic order of relationships in and among schools and the communities they serve, we can begin to focus, as Du Bois first suggested, not on whether the Negro child, or any child, needs segregated schools or mixed schools, but how we can ensure every child receives *an education.*

In answering Dr. King's call to become firefighters and respond to the persistent moral dilemma of race in the United States, we can begin to advance equal education through racial literacy, racial realism, racial reconstruction, and racial reconciliation in order to foster an atmosphere of healing and harmony that counteracts the forces of disintegration that, if left unattended, will jeopardize any effort to advance social justice in schools. Through community engagement, political activism, and the building of sustainable cross-racial coalitions committed to restoring a moral and ethical commitment to equal education, we can work to transform the systems and structures that have abdicated responsibility for the educational experiences of our nation's schoolchildren so that no child will learn in a burning house.

Learning in the World House

> We have inherited a large house, a great "world house" in which we have to live together . . . a family unduly separated in ideas, culture and interests, who, because we can never again live apart, must learn somehow to live with each other in peace.
>
> —Dr. Martin Luther King, Jr.,
> *Where Do We Go From Here: Chaos or Community?* 1968

Major events in the United States in recent years have reinforced the notion of interdependence among individuals, organizations, and the countries of our world. From the terrorist attacks of September 11, 2001, and the largest economic recession recorded in U.S. history, to social networking and the 24-hour news cycle, the realities of the 21st century reflect the internationalization and globalization Dr. Martin Luther King, Jr., spoke of 47 years ago. In his Nobel Lecture of December 11, 1964, which later was published as a book chapter entitled "The World House," Dr. King declared, "All inhabitants of the globe are now neighbors" (p. 3). He predicted the continued development in the areas of science, medicine, and technology; of "automation" and "cybernation" that would forever change the ways in which we work and play not only in the United States, but also in the rest of the world.

His remarks focused heavily on our nation's failure to address issues of poverty, economic exploitation, and increased militarization—the very same issues plaguing our nation today in what author Thomas Friedman (2007) popularly characterized as an increasingly "flat world." In the field of education, Linda Darling-Hammond's (2010) extensive examination, discussion, and action plan of what must happen in U.S. public education to re-establish our position in the world underscore both the realities of our changing world and how we must proceed to ensure we provide a high-quality, equitable education for all of our nation's children. Indeed, the current discourse on internationalization and globalization in education underscores Dr. King's prophetic declaration concerning the need "to achieve the new attitudes and the new mental outlooks that the new situation demands." For not only did he characterize the intersection of poverty, racism, economic exploitation, and war as a "burning house," but he located these injustices within a much broader context—the "world house"—reminding us:

> Today our survival depends on our ability to stay awake, to adjust to new ideas, to remain vigilant and to face the challenge of change. The large house in which we live demands that we transform this world-wide neighborhood into a world-wide brotherhood. Together we must learn to live as brothers or together we will be forced to perish as fools. (p. x)

The choice is clear. Given the progress in social relations that has been made since Dr. King's clarion call to "learn somehow to live to together in peace," I argue in this chapter that we must grab hold of the distinct opportunities and capabilities that our increasingly international and global contexts have to offer us. We are no longer separated by distance and time. Rather than continuing along the path of schooling and education as usual, we must adopt and pursue a moral vision of education that prepares our children for leadership and lifelong learning in this world house.

THE DEATH OF DISTANCE:
PREPARING GLOBAL CITIZENS THROUGH EDUCATION

In his book, *Leading up or Catching the Way*, Zhao (2009) depicts this flattening of the world through increased globalization and technological advances as the "death of distance" and challenges schools to become "global enterprises" that support creativity and better prepare students to become global citizens in a multicultural and diverse world (Banks, 1997, 2007; Murakami-Ramalho, 2009). Zhao gives an account of how, in one 24-hour period, he effectively was in physical or virtual contact with individuals from 20 countries across the world. In fact, his narrative reflects Dr. King's notion of interconnectedness in the world house, for as Zhao explained, "My well-being, both psychological and physical, was taken care of by these individuals, and my action as a consumer had in some way affected them as well" (p. 98). And while notions of Marshall McLuhan's (1964) "global village" and more recently, Thomas Friedman's (2005) "flat world" have been particularly significant as they relate to the economy and commerce, the realities of globalization and internationalization continue to become increasingly critical to the study and practice of education. In fact, we must consider ways to globalize curriculum, content, and staff to not only enrich the quality of learning experienced by students in schools, but also address the growing concern of an international achievement gap, which can be mitigated in many important ways through equitable pedagogical and leadership practices.

Arguably, this expanded approach to education would not only narrow the growing gap in comparative international education, but also allow students who have been unfairly and historically disadvantaged and underserved in our nation's schools to enjoy the success that naturally flows from their unique skills, gifts, and talents—many of which go unnoticed, unmeasured, and unvalued through standardization, centralization, and high-stakes accountability contexts. As Dr. King (1968) declared, "Equality with whites will not solve the problems of either whites nor Negroes if it means equality in a world society stricken by poverty and in a universe doomed to extinction by war" (p. 3).

The real challenge we face is the discomfort and apprehension of leaders who are reluctant to step back and search the oft-cited "problem," "challenge," or "issue" of inequality, injustice, inequity, and iniquity as it concerns the future of education for a growing percentage of our nation's children and youth. It is a moral challenge. But it's not enough to simply revisit the problem. Maybe the fact that we have chosen to observe, analyze, and even admire the problem of educational inequality is where the problem takes root. Perhaps it is time to stop investigating and interrogating, and rather listen with our hearts and minds and heed the call for moral and just leadership.

IMPROVED MEANS TO AN IMPROVED END: ALIGNING MEANINGFUL GOALS TO MEANINGFUL OUTCOMES

It seems our inability to acknowledge and embrace this shared space—this world house—particularly in education, has been fueled by and resulted in ideologies, policies, and programs that have demonstrated our fate to perish as fools. Like clear air and clean water, most Americans support education, but disagreement surrounding the purpose of public education, how it should be delivered, to what degree it should be funded, and whom it should serve, remains as contentious as any other ideological debate. The politicization of education has resulted in a high-stakes accountability culture, and in some cases privatization of public schools that distract efforts from meaningful systemic education reform. Our children have become commodities and a means to an end, rather than an opportunity to improve an educational end.

Will shutting down "persistently underachieving schools" for failing to meet "adequate yearly progress," after firing all the administrators and teaching staff, get us there? Will allowing teachers who blame and shame children of color and children of poverty to continue to harm children, and failing to provide them with proper training and continued professional development and support get us there? Will turning a blind eye to the social forces of unemployment, racism, and violence and their impact on schooling get us there? Will maintaining a greater concern for the rights and protections of adults over those of our children get us there? What about the children? How are the children? And how do we care for, educate, and nurture our children so that they can reach their highest potential (Walker, 1996) in this world house?

While we have worked feverishly to perfect the accountability systems, tests, metrics, and programs designed to "improve education," we have sorely missed important opportunities to define what we mean by the purpose of education and, in turn, how to improve and enhance that end (Ravitch, 2010). Indeed, federal and state education policy initiatives continue to "value what we measure" rather than "measure what we value" (Guinier, 2006)—a lack of moral vision that arguably has undermined educational quality and equality in the United States. While nations such as China, India, Singapore, and the others we strive to emulate educationally are investing in strategies that advance creativity and maximize the unique talents, gifts, and abilities of their citizens, we remain committed to doing the opposite (Zhao, 2009).

OUR GREAT INHERITANCE: LEARNING IN THE WORLD HOUSE

As Dr. King (1968) warned:

> Our hope for creative living in this world house that we have inherited lies in our ability to re-establish the moral ends of our lives in personal character and social justice. Without this spiritual and moral awakening we shall destroy ourselves in the misuse of our own instruments. (p. 6)

While he clearly was speaking against war and misguided missiles, he also spoke of misguided men, and perhaps this is why a moral vision for education that prepares children to live in a world house that values equality, peace, and justice is essential to the future of the field and our world. We no longer can blame or shame children for not taking ownership of or self-investment in their education. It is time for us to accept the fact that the challenges facing education are not child problems, but adult problems (Edelman, 2008). We are the ones who hold the power, the ability, and potential to either destroy or invest in our children, whom President John F. Kennedy characterized as "our world's greatest resource" and "our best hope for the future."

How will we choose to educate and prepare our greatest resource and best hope for the future in the world house? We have not done the best job in times past, sanctioning and maintaining separate worlds through separate schools. Strategically choosing to desegregate with all deliberate speed and finding creative ways to exhibit proximity, but never affinity. Witnessing, and in many instances facilitating, the disintegration of the integration ideal while constructing an illusion of Black progress and inclusion only to measure and, even worse, expect the same gaps and disparities by race and poverty. And if we choose colorblindness over color consciousness, we will continue to limit our ability to *see* and benefit from the fullness of our inheritance—a global village rich with diverse experiences, perspectives, human capital, and resources necessary for creative living and learning in the world house.

We must be good stewards of this inheritance. By building on the knowledge of the history of discrimination in U.S. education, the intended and unintended consequences of segregation and desegregation, and the struggle for equal education that determinedly and effectively has sought to "Americanize America," we are better prepared than ever before to advance the true goal of meaningful integration—a community founded on mutual respect where we do not lose who we are, but share who we are (Edelman, 2008).

Together, we can transform our school communities, our nation, and the world, ensuring that desegregation is no longer a joke, or equal education a sagging dream. That from this burning house, we can rise from the ashes and rebuild a beloved community. Teaching, leading, and learning in the world house. A place everyone can call home.

References

Adair, A. V. (1984). *Desegregation: The illusion of black progress.* New York: University Press of America.

Adelman, L. (Producer). (2003). *Race: The power of an illusion* [Motion picture]. San Francisco: California Newsreel.

African American Students and U.S. High Schools. (September 2008). Fact Sheet. Alliance for Excellent Education. Retrieved October 19, 2010, from http://www.all4ed.org/publication_material/fact_sheets?page=1

Afrik, M. H. T. (1993). The future of Afrikan American education: A practitioner's view. Paper presented at the annual meeting of the American Educational Research Association, April 15, in Atlanta. http://www.nbufront.org/html/FRONTalView/ArticlesPapers/hannibal1.html (accessed April 12, 2007).

Alemán, E., Jr. (2007). Situating Texas school finance policy in a CRT framework: How "substantially equal" yields racial inequity. *Educational Administration Quarterly, 43*(5), 525–558.

Alemán, E., Jr. (2010). The politics of equity, adequacy, and educational leadership in a (post)racial America. In S. D. Horsford (Ed.), *New perspectives in educational leadership: Exploring social, political, and community contexts and meaning* (pp. 127–152). New York: Peter Lang.

Alexander, K., & Alexander, M. D. (2001). *American public school law* (5th ed.). Belmont, CA: Wadsworth/Thomson Learning.

Alliance for Excellent Education. (September 2008). *African American students and U.S. high schools.* Retrieved October 19, 2010, from http://www.all4ed.org/publication_material/fact_sheets?page=1

Alvarez, R. R., Jr. (1986). The Lemon Grove incident: The nation's first successful desegregation court case. *The Journal of San Diego History, 32*(2), 116–135.

America's Cradle to Prison Pipeline®: A Children's Defense Fund Report (2007). Washington, DC: Children's Defense Fund.

A Nation at Risk. (1983). Retrieved November 2, 2010, from http://www2.ed.gov/pubs/NatAtRisk/index.html

Anderson, J. D. (1988). *The education of Blacks in the South, 1860–1935.* Chapel Hill: University of North Carolina Press.

Anderson, J. D. (2007). Race-conscious educational policies versus a "color-blind constitution": A historical perspective. *Educational Researcher, 36*(5), 249–257.

Anyon, J. (1997). *Ghetto schooling: A political economy of urban educational reform.* New York: Teachers College Press.

Artiles, A. J. (2003). Special education's changing identity: Paradoxes and dilem-mas in views of culture and space. *Harvard Educational Review, 73*(2), 164–186.

Artiles, A. J., Trent, S. C., & Palmer, J. (2004). Culturally diverse students in spe-cial education: Legacies and prospects. In J. A. Banks & C. M. Banks (Eds.), *Handbook of research on multicultural education* (2nd ed.) (pp. 716–735). San Francisco: Jossey-Bass.

Banks, J. A. (1997). *Educating citizens in a multicultural society.* New York: Teachers College Press.

Banks, J. A. (Ed.). (2007). *Diversity and citizenship education: Global perspectives.* San Franciso: Jossey-Bass.

Beachum, F. D., & McCray, C. R. (2004, September 14). Cultural collision in urban schools. *Current Issues in Education, 7(5).* Available online: http://cie.ed.asu.edu/volume7/number5/

Beachum F. D., & McCray, C. R. (2008). Dealing with cultural collision in urban schools: What pre-service educators should know. In G. S. Goodman (Ed.), *Education Psychology: An application of critical constructivism.* New York: Peter Lang.

Beauboeuf-Lafontant, T. (2002). A womanist experience of caring: Understand-ing the pedagogy of exemplary Black women teachers. *The Urban Review, 34,* 71–86.

Bell, D. (1976). Serving two masters: Integration ideals and client interests in school desegregation litigation. *The Yale Law Journal, 85,* 470–516.

Bell, D. (Ed.). (1980a). Brown v. Board of Education and the interest convergence dilemma. *Harvard Law Review, 93,* 518–533.

Bell, D. (Ed.). (1980b). *Shades of Brown: New perspectives on school desegregation.* New York: Teachers College Press.

Bell, D. (1992). *Faces at the bottom of the well: The permanence of racism.* New York: Basic Books.

Bell, D. (1995). *Brown v. Board of Education* and the interest convergence dilemma. In K. Crenshaw, N. Gotanda, G. Peller, & K. Thomas (Eds.), *Critical race theory: They key writings that formed the movement* (pp. 20–28). New York: The New Press.

Bell, D. (2004). *Silent covenants: Brown v. Board of Education and the unfulfilled hopes for racial reform.* New York: Oxford University Press.

Berea College v. Kentucky, 211 U.S. 45 (1908).

Board of Education of Oklahoma City v. Dowell, 498 U.S. 237 (1991).

Boger, J. C., & Orfield, G. (Eds.). (2005). *School resegregation: Must the South turn back?* Chapel Hill: University of North Carolina Press.

Bonilla-Silva, E. (2006). *Racism without racists: Color-blind racism and the persistence of racial inequality in the United States.* (2nd ed.). Lanham, MD: Rowman & Littlefield.

Boykin, A. W. (1986). The triple quandary and the schooling of Afro-American children. In U. Neisser (Ed.), *The school achievement of minority children: New perspectives* (pp. 57–92). Hillsdale, NJ: Erlbaum.

Brooks, J. S., & Miles, M. T. (2010). Educational leadership and the shaping of school culture: Classic concepts and cutting-edge possibilities. In *New perspec-tives in educational leadership: Exploring social, political, and community contexts and meaning* (pp. 7–28). New York: Peter Lang.

Brown v. Board of Education of Topeka, Kansas (Brown I), 347 U.S. 483 (1954).

Brown v. Board of Education of Topeka, Kansas (Brown II), 349 U.S. 284 (1955).

Cashin, S. (2004). *The failures of integration: How race and class are undermining the American Dream.* New York: PublicAffairs.

Children's Defense Fund. (2008). *The state of America's children 2008.* Retrieved September 5, 2010, from http://www.childrensdefense.org/child-research-data-publications/data/state-of-americas-children-2008-report.html

Clark, K. B. (1965). *Dark ghetto: Dilemmas of social power.* New York: Harper & Row.

Clark, K. B. (1995). *Beyond Brown v. Board of Education: Housing and education in the year 2000.* Keynote Address. Institute on Race & Poverty. Retrieved January 28, 2007, from http://www1.umn.edu/irp/publications/linking.htm#clark

Clotfelter, C. T., Vigdor, J. L., & Ladd, H. F. (Eds.). (2006). Federal oversight, local control, and the specter of "resegregation" in Southern schools. *American Law and Economics Review, 8*(2), 347–389.

Coleman, J. (1966). *Equality of educational opportunity.* U.S. Department of Health, Education and Welfare. Washington DC: U.S. Printing Office.

Cox, O. C. (1948). *Caste, class, and race.* New York: Doubleday.

Crenshaw, K. (1988). Race, reform, and retrenchment: Transformation and legitimation in antidiscrimination law. *Harvard Law Review, 101,* 1331.

Crenshaw, K. W. (1995). Mapping the margins: Intersectionality, identity politics, and violence against women of color. In K. Crenshaw, N. Gotanda, G. Peller, & K. Thomas (Eds.), *Critical race theory: The key writings that formed the movement* (pp. 357–383). New York: New Press.

Cumming v. Board of Education of Richmond County, 175 U.S. 528 (1899).

Dancy, T. E., & Horsford, S. D. (2010). Considering the social context of school and campus communities: The importance of culturally proficient leadership. In *New perspectives in educational leadership: Exploring social, political, and community contexts and meaning* (pp. 153–171). New York: Peter Lang.

Dantley, M., & Tillman, L. C. (2006). Social justice and moral transformative leadership. In C. Marshall & M. Oliva (Eds.), *Leadership for social justice: Making revolutions in education* (pp. 16–30). Boston: Pearson.

Darling-Hammond, L. (2004). Inequality and the right to learn: Access to qualified teachers in California's Public Schools. *Teachers College Record, 106*(10), 1936–1966.

DeCuir, J. T., & Dixson, A. D. (2004). "So when it comes out, they aren't that surprised that it is there": Using critical race theory as a tool of analysis of race and racism in education. *Educational Researcher, 33*(5), 26–31.

Delgado, R., & Stefancic, J. (Eds.). (2000). *Critical race theory: The cutting edge* (2nd ed.). Philadelphia: Temple University Press.

Delgado, R., & Stefancic, J. (Eds.). (2001). *Critical race theory: An introduction.* New York: New York University Press.

Delpit, L. (2001). *Other people's children: Cultural conflict in the classroom.* New York: New Press.

Dempsey, V., & Noblit, G. W. (1993). The demise of caring in an African American community: One consequence of school desegregation. *The Urban Review, 25*(1), 47–61.

Dixson, A. D., & Dingus, J. (2008). In search of our mother's gardens: Black women teachers and professional socialization. *Teachers College Record, 110*(4), 805–837.

Dixson, A. D., & Rousseau, C. K. (2005). And we are still not saved: critical race theory in education ten years later. *Race Ethnicity and Education, 8*(1), 7–27.

Douglass, F. (1883). Address to the Louisville Convention. Retrieved October 19, 2010, from http://home.flash.net/~ccarney/douglasslouisville.htm

D'Souza, D. (1995). *The end of racism: Principles for a multiracial society.* New York: Simon & Schuster.

Du Bois, W. E. B. (1935). *Black reconstruction in America.* New York: Harcourt, Brace.

Du Bois, W. E. B. (1935). Does the Negro need separate schools? *Journal of Negro Education, 4*(3), 328–335.

Duncan, A. (2010, March 8). Crossing the next bridge: Secretary Arne Duncan's Remarks on the 45th Anniversary of "Bloody Sunday" at the Edmund Pettus Bridge, Selma, Alabama. Retrieved September 15, 2010, from http://www.ed.gov/news/speeches/crossing-next-bridge-secretary-arne-duncan%E2%80%99s-remarks-45th-anniversary-bloody-sunday-ed

Dunn, L. M. (1968). Special education for the mildly retarded—is much of it justifiable? *Exceptional Children, 35,* 0–22.

Dyson, M. E. (2008, November 5). Race, post race: Barack Obama's historic victory represents a quantum leap in the racial progress of the United States. *Los Angeles Times.* Retrieved June 11, 2009, from http://www.latimes.com

Edelman, M. W. (2008). *The sea is so wide and my boat is so small: Charting a course for the next generation* New York: Hyperion.

Ethridge, S. (1979). Impact of the 1954 *Brown vs. Topeka Board of Education* decision on Black educators. *Negro Educational Review, 30,* 217–232.

Eyler, J., Cook, V., & Ward, L. (1983). Resegregation: Segregation within desegregated schools. In C. H. Rossell & W. D. Hawley (Eds.), *The consequences of school desegregation* (pp. 126–210). Philadelphia: Temple University Press.

Fairclough, A. (2004). The costs of *Brown*: Black teachers and school integration. *The Journal of American History, 91*(1), 43–55.

Faltz, C. J., & Leake, D. O. (1996). The all-Black school: Inherently unequal or a culture- based alternative? In M. J. Shujaa (Ed.), *Beyond desegregation: The politics of quality in African American schooling.* Thousand Oaks, CA: Corwin.

Foner, E., & Mahoney, O. (1990). *A house divided: America in the age of Lincoln.* Chicago: Chicago Historical Society.

Fordham, S., & Ogbu, J. (1986). Black students' school success: Coping with the burden of "acting White." *The Urban Review, 18*(3), 176–206.

Foster, L. (2005). The practice of educational leadership in African American communities of learning: Context, scope, and meaning. *Educational Administration Quarterly, 41*(4), 689–700.

Foster, M. (1997). *Black teachers on teaching.* New York: New Press.

Franklin, J. H. & Moss, A., Jr. (1988). *From slavery to freedom: A history of Negro Americans.* (6th ed.). New York: McGraw-Hill.

Fuller, B., Elmore, R. F., & Orfield, G. (Eds.). (1996). *Who chooses? Who loses?: Cul-*

ture, institutions, and the unequal effects of school choice. New York: Teachers College Press.

Gay, G. (2000). *Culturally responsive teaching: Theory, research, and practice.* New York: Teachers College Press.

Gay, G. (2002). Culturally responsive teaching in special education for ethnically diverse students: Setting the stage. *International Journal of Qualitative Studies in Education, 15*(6), 613–629.

Gong Lum v. Rice, 275 U.S. 78 (1927).

Gordon, R., Paina, L., & Keleher, T. (2000). *Suspension, expulsions, and zero tolerance policies.* Oakland, CA: Applied Research Center.

Gotanda, N. (1991). A critique of "Our constitution is color-blind." *Stanford Law Review, 44,* 1–68.

Green v. County School Board of New Kent County, 391 U.S. 430 (1968).

Guinier, L. (2006). From racial liberalism to racial literacy: *Brown v. Board of Education* and the interest-divergence dilemma. *The Journal of American History, 91*(1), 92–118.

Guinier, L., & Torres, G. (2002). *The miner's canary: Enlisting race, resisting power, transforming democracy.* Cambridge, MA: Harvard University Press.

Hale-Benson, J. (1986). *Black children: Their roots culture and learning styles* (Rev. ed.). Baltimore: The Johns Hopkins University Press.

Harris, C. I. (1995). Whiteness as property. In K. Crenshaw, N. Gotanda, G. Peller, & K. Thomas (Eds.), *Critical race theory: The key writings that formed the movement* (pp. 276–291). New York: New Press.

Hernandez v. Texas, 347 U.S. 475 (1954).

Hilliard, A. G. (1967). Cross-cultural teaching. *Journal of Teacher Education, 18*(1), 32–35.

Hilliard, A. G. (2003). No mystery: Closing the achievement gap between Africans and excellence. In T. Perry, C. Steele, & A. G. Hilliard (Eds.), Young, gifted, and Black: Promoting high achievement among African-American students (pp. 131–183). Boston: Beacon Press.

Holzman, M. (2006). *Public education and Black male students: The 2006 state report card.* Schott Educational Inequity Index. Cambridge, MA: Schott Foundation for Public Education.

Horsford, S. D. (2007). Vestiges of desegregation: Black superintendent reflections on the complex legacy of *Brown v. Board of Education. Dissertation Abstracts International, A68* (4).

Horsford, S. D. (2008). A history of school desegregation in the "Mississippi of the West": Implications for educational leaders. UCEA Conference Proceedings for Convention 2008.

Horsford, S. D. (2009a). From *Negro* student to *Black* superintendent: Counternarratives on segregation and desegregation. *The Journal of Negro Education, 78*(2), 172–187.

Horsford, S. D. (2009b). The case for racial literacy in educational leadership: Lessons learned from superintendent reflections on desegregation. *UCEA Review, 50*(2), 5–8.

Horsford, S. D. (2010a). Black superintendents on educating Black students in separate and unequal contexts: *The Urban Review, 42*(1), 58–79.

Horsford, S. D. (2010b). Mixed feelings about mixed schools: Superintendents on the complex legacy of school desegregation. *Educational Administration Quarterly, 46*(3), 287–321.

Horsford, S. D., & McKenzie, K. B. (2008). "Sometimes I feel like the problems started with desegregation": Exploring Black superintendent perspectives on desegregation policy. *International Journal of Qualitative Studies in Education, 21*(5), 443–455.

Hudson, M. J., & Holmes, B. J. (1994). Missing teachers, impaired communities: The unanticipated consequences of *Brown v. Board of Education* on the African American teaching force at the precollegiate level. *Journal of Negro Education, 63,* 388–393.

Hunter, R. C., & Donahoo, S. (2005). All things to all people: Special circumstances influencing the performance of African American superintendents. *Education and Urban Society, 37*(4), 419–430.

Irons, J. (2002). *Jim Crow's children: The broken promise of the Brown decision.* New York: Viking.

Irvine, J. J. (1991). *Black students and school failure: Policies, practices, and prescriptions.* Westport, NY: Praeger.

Jackson, B. L. (2008). Race, education, and the politics of fear. *Educational Policy, 22*(1), 130–154.

Jencks, C., & Phillips, M. (Eds). (1998*). The Black-White test score gap.* Washington ,DC: Brookings Institution Press.

Jones, F. (1981). The *traditional model of excellence: Dunbar High School in Little Rock, Arkansas.* Washington, DC: Howard University Press.

King, J. E. (Ed.). (2005). *Black education: A transformative research and action agenda for the new century.* New York: Routledge.

King, M. L. (1968). *Where do we go from here: Chaos or community?* New York: Bantam Books.

King, M. L. (1986). The ethical demands for integration In J. M. Washington (Ed.), *A testament of hope: The essential writings and speeches of Martin Luther King, Jr.* (pp. 117–125). New York: HarperCollins. (Original work published 1962)

Kozol, J. (1991). *Savage Inequalities: Children in America's schools.* New York: Crown.

Kozol, J. (2005). *The shame of the nation: The restoration of apartheid schooling in America.* New York: Crown.

Ladson-Billings, G. (1994*). The dreamkeepers: Successful teachers of African American children.* San Francisco: Jossey-Bass.

Ladson-Billings, G. (1998). Just what is critical race theory and what's it doing in a *nice* field like education? *International Journal of Qualitative Studies in Education, 11,* 7–24.

Ladson-Billings, G. (2004). Landing on the wrong note: The price we paid for *Brown. Educational Researche*r, *33*(7), 3–13.

Ladson-Billings, G. (2005). The evolving role of critical race theory in educational scholarship. *Race, Ethnicity and Education, 8*(1), 115–119.

Ladson-Billings, G. (2010). "The Social Funding of Race." Plenary Session I. 4th Annual Critical Race Studies in Education Conference. Salt Lake City, Utah.

Ladson-Billings, G., & Tate, W. F. (1995). Toward a critical race theory of education. *Teachers College Record, 97*(1), 47–68.

Leonardo, Z. (Ed.). (2005). *Critical pedagogy and race.* Malden, MA: Blackwell.

Lightfoot, S. L. (1980). Families as educators: The forgotten people of *Brown.* In D. Bell (Ed.), *Shades of Brown: New perspectives on school desegregation* (pp. 3–19). New York: Teachers College Press.

Loder, T. (2005). African American women principals' reflections on social change, community othermothering, and Chicago Public School Reform. *Urban Education, 40*(3), 298–320.

Loewen, J. W. (2005). *Sundown towns: A hidden dimension of American racism.* New York: Simon & Schuster.

Lomotey, K. (Ed.). (1990). *Going to school: The African American experience.* Albany: State University of New York Press.

Lopez, G. R. (2003). The (racially neutral) politics of education: A critical race theory perspective. *Educational Administration Quarterly, 39*(1), 68–94.

Lopez, G. R., & Parker, L. (Eds.). (2003). *Interrogating racism in qualitative research methodology.* New York: Peter Lang.

Lynn, M., & Parker, L. (2006). Critical race studies in education: Examining a decade of research on U.S. schools. *Urban Review: Issues and Ideas in Public Education, 38*(4), 257–290.

Marshall, C., & Oliva, M. (2010). *Leadership for social justice: Making revolutions in education.* (3rd ed.). Prentice Hall.

Matsuda, M. (1995). Looking to the bottom: Critical legal studies and reparations. In K. Crenshaw, N. Gotanda, G. Peller, & K. Thomas (Eds.), *Critical race theory: The key writings that formed the movement* (pp. 63–79). New York: New Press.

McKenzie, K. B. (2009). Emotional abuse of students of color: The hidden inhumanity in our schools. *International Journal of Qualitative Studies in Education, 22*(2), 129–143.

McLuhan, M. (1964). *Understanding media: The extension of man.* New York: McGraw Hill.

Meier, K. J., Stewart, J., & England R. E. (1989). *Race, class, and education: The politics of second-generation discrimination.* Madison: The University of Wisconsin Press.

Mickelson, R. A. (2001). Subverting Swann: First- and second-generation segregation in the Charlotte-Mecklenburg schools. *American Educational Research Journal, 38,* 215–252.

Mickelson, R. A. (2005). How tracking undermines race equity in desegregated schools. In J. Petrovich and A. S. Wells (Eds.), *Bringing equity back: Research for a new era in American educational policy* (pp. 49–76). New York: Teachers College Press.

Mickelson, R. A., & Heath, D. (1999). The effects of segregation and tracking on African American high school seniors' academic achievement. *Journal of Negro Education, 68*(4), 566–586.

Minow, M. (2008). After *Brown:* What would Martin Luther King Say? *Lewis & Clark Law Review 12,* 599–647.

Missouri ex. rel Gaines v. Canada, 305 U.S. 337 (1938).

Moody, C. D. (1971). *Black superintendents in public school districts: Trends and conditions.* Unpublished dissertation, Northwestern University, Evanston, IL.

Morris, J. E. (1999). A pillar of strength: An African American school's communal bonds with families and community since Brown. *Urban Education, 33*(5),
584–605.

Morris, J. E. (2001). Forgotten voices of Black educators: Critical race perspectives on the implementation of a desegregation plan. *Educational Policy, 15*(4),
575–600.

Morris, J. E. (2008). Research, ideology, and the *Brown* decision: Counter-narratives
to the historical and contemporary representation of Black schooling. *Teachers
College Record, 110*(4), 713–732.

Morris, J. E. (2009). *Troubling the waters: Fulfilling the promise of quality public schooling for Black children.* New York: Teachers College Press.

Murakami-Ramalho, E. (2010). Educational leadership in a changing world: Preparing students for internationalization and globalization through advocacy
leadership. In S. D. Horsford (Ed.), *New perspectives in educational leadership: Exploring social, political, and community contexts and meaning* (pp. 197–214). New
York: Peter Lang.

Murtadha, K., & Watts, D. M. (2005). Linking the struggle for education and social justice: Historical perspectives of African American leadership in schools.
Educational Administration Quarterly, 41(4), 591–608.

National Alliance of Black School Educators. (2010). Education is a civil right.
Retrieved September 12, 2010, from http://www.nabse.org/civilright.html

National Center for Child Poverty Website. (2010). Retrieved September 5, 2010,
at http://www.nccp.org/topics/childpoverty.html

No Child Left Behind Act of 2001, 20 U.S.C. § 6319

Noguera, P. (2008). *The trouble with black boys: And other reflections on race, equity, and
the future of public education.* San Francisco: Jossey-Bass.

Oakes, J. (1986). *Keeping track: How schools structure inequality.* New Haven: Yale
University Press.

Oakes, J. (1995). Two cities' tracking and within-school segregation. *Teachers College Record, 96*(4), 681–690.

Oakes, J., Wells, A. S., Jones, M., & Datnow, A. (1997). Detracking: The social
construction of ability, cultural politics, and resistance to reform. *Teachers College Record, 98*(3), 482–510.

Ogbu, J. (2003). *Black American students in an affluent suburb: A study of academic
disengagement.* Hillsdale, NJ: Erlbaum.

Ogletree, C. J. (2004). *All deliberate speed: Reflections on the first half-century of Brown
v. Board of Education.* New York: W.W. Norton & Company.

Olivas, M.A. (Ed.). (2006). *Colored men and hombres aqui:* Hernandez v. Texas *and
the emergence of Mexican-American lawyering.* Houston: Arte Público Press.

Omi, M., & Winant, H. (1986). *Racial formation in the United States: From the 1960s to
the 1980s.* New York & London: Routledge.

Orfield, G. (1996). Toward an integrated future: New directions for courts, educators, civil rights groups, policymakers, and scholars. In G. Orfield & S. Eaton
(Eds.), *Dismantling desegregation: The quiet reversal* of Brown v. Board of Education (pp. 331–361). New York: Free Press.

Orfield, G. (2005). The southern dilemma: Losing *Brown,* fearing *Plessy.* In J. C.
Boger & G. Orfield (Eds.), *School resegregation: Must the South turn back?* (pp.

1–25). Chapel Hill: University of North Carolina Press.

Orfield, G. (2009). *Reviving the goal of an integrated society: A 21st century challenge.* Los Angeles, CA: The Civil Rights Project/Proyecto Derechos Civiles at UCLA.

Orfield, G., & Eaton, S. (Eds.). (1996). *Dismantling desegregation: The quiet reversal of Brown v. Board of Education.* New York: New Press.

Orfield, G., & Lee, C. (2004). Brown *at 50: King's dream or Plessy's nightmare?* Retrieved October 15, 2010 from http://www.eric.ed.gov/PDFS/ED489168.pdf

Parents Involved in Community Schools v. Seattle School District No. 1, et al., 551 U.S. (2007).

Parker, L. (1998). "Race is, race isn't": An exploration of the utility of critical race theory in qualitative research in education. *International Journal of Qualitative Studies in Education, 11*(1), 43–55.

Parker, L. (2003). Critical race theory and its implications for methodology and policy analysis in higher education desegregation. In G. R. Lopez & L. Parker (Eds.), *Interrogating racism in qualitative research methodology* (pp. 145–180). New York: Peter Lang.

Parker, L., Deyhle, D., & Villenas, S. (Eds.). (1999). *Race is . . . race isn't: Critical race theory and qualitative studies in education.* Boulder, CO: Westview Press.

Parker, L., & Lynn, M. (2002). What's race got to do with it? Critical race theory's conflicts with and connections to qualitative research methodology and epistemology. *Qualitative Inquiry, 8*(1), 7–22.

Parker, L., & Villalpondo, O. (2007). A race(cialized) perspective on education leadership: Critical race theory in educational administration. *Educational Administration Quarterly, 43*(5), 519–524.

Perkins, L. (1989). The history of Blacks in teaching. In D. Warren (Ed.), American teachers: History of a profession at work (pp.344–367). New York: Macmillan.

Pillow, W. (2003). Race-based methodologies: Multicultural methods or epistemological shifts? In Lopez & Parker (Eds.), *Interrogating racism in qualitative research methodology.* New York: Peter Lang.

Plessy v. Ferguson, 163 U.S. 537 (1896).

Pollard, D.S., & Ajirotutu, C. S. (Eds.). (2000). *African-centered schooling in theory and practice.* Westport, CT: Bergin & Garvey.

Ravitch, D. (1980). Desegregation: Varieties of meaning. In D. Bell (Ed.), *Shades of Brown: New perspectives on school desegregation* (pp. 31–47). New York: Teachers College Press.

Ravitch, D. (2010). *The death and life of the great American school system: How testing and choice are undermining education.* New York: Basic Books.

The Rise and Fall of Jim Crow [film]. (2010). http://www.pbs.org/wnet/jimcrow/stories_events_segregation.html

Roberts v. City of Boston, 59 Mass. 198 (1848–49).

Rodgers, F. (1967). *The black high school and its community.* Lexington, MA: Lexington Books.

Roithmayr, D. (1999). Introduction to critical race theory in educational research and praxis. In L. Parker, D. Deyhle, & S. Villenas (Eds.), *Race is . . . race isn't: Critical race theory and qualitative studies in education* (pp. 1–6). Boulder, CO: Westview Press.

Rusch, E. A., & Horsford, S. D. (2009). Changing hearts and minds: The quest for open talk about race in educational leadership. *International Journal of Educational Management, 23*(4), 302–313.

Scheurich, J. J., & Young, M. D. (1997). Coloring epistemologies: Are our research epistemologies racially biased? *Educational Researcher, 26*(4), 4–16.

Scott, H. J. (1980). *The Black school superintendent: Messiah or scapegoat?* Washington, DC: Howard University Press.

Scott, H. J. (1983). View of black school superintendents on school desegregation. *Journal of Negro Education, 52*(4), 378–382.

Shujaa, M. J. (Ed.). (1996). *Beyond desegregation: The politics of quality in African American schooling.* Thousand Oaks, CA: Corwin Press.

Skrla, L., McKenzie, K., & Scheurich, J. (2008). *Equity audits: Leadership tool for developing equitable and excellent schools.* Thousand Oaks. CA: Corwin.

Solórzano, D. G., & Yosso, T. J. (2002). A critical race counterstory of race, racism, and affirmative action. *Equity & Excellence in Education, 35*(2), 155–168.

Sotero, M. M. (2006). A conceptual model of historical trauma: Implications for public health practice and research. *Journal of Health Disparities Research and Practice, 1*(1), 93–108.

Steele, S. (2008, November 5). Obama's post-racial promise. *Los Angeles Times.* Retrieved June 11, 2009, from http://www.latimes.com

Sturm, S., & Guinier, L. (2000). The future of affirmative action. *Boston Review.* Retrieved September 15, 2010, from http://bostonreview.net/BR25.6/sturm/html.

Sugrue, T. J. (2008). *Sweet land of liberty: The forgotten struggle for civil rights in the North.* New York: Random House.

Sweatt v. Painter, 339 U.S. 629 (1950).

Takaki, R. (1993). *A different mirror: A history of multicultural America.* Boston: Back Bay Books.

Tamura, E. H. (Ed.). (2008). *The history of discrimination in U.S. education: Marginality, agency, and power.* New York: Palgrave Macmillan.

Tate, W. (1997). Critical race theory and education: History, theory and implications. *Review of Research in Education, 22,* 195–247.

Tate, W. F., Ladson-Billings, G., & Grant, C. A. (1996). The *Brown* decision revisited: Mathematizing a social problem. In M. J. Shujaa (Ed.), *Beyond desegregation: The politics of quality in African American schooling* (pp. 29–50). Thousand Oaks, CA: Corwin Press.

Tatum, B. D. (2007). *Can we talk about race? And other conversations in an era of school resegregation.* Boston: Beacon Press.

Taylor, E. (1998). A primer on critical race theory: Who are the critical race theorists and what are they saying? *Journal of Blacks in Higher Education, 19,* 122–124.

Tillman, L. (2002). Culturally sensitive research approaches: An African-American perspective. *Educational Researcher, 31,* 3–12.

Tillman, L. (2004a). African American principals and the legacy of *Brown. Review of Research in Education, 28,* 101–146.

Tillman, L. (2004b). (Un)intended consequences? The impact of *Brown v. Board of Education* decision on the employment status of Black educators. *Education and Urban Society, 36*(3), 280–303.

Tillman, L. (2008). The scholarship of Dr. Asa G. Hilliard, III: Implications for Black principal leadership. *Review of Research in Education, 73*(3), 589–607.

Valenzuela, A. (1999). *Subtractive schooling: U.S.-Mexican youth and the politics of caring.* New York: State University of New York Press.

Walker, V. S. (1996). *Their highest potential: An African American school community in the segregated South.* Chapel Hill: University of North Carolina Press.

Walker, V. S. (2000). Valued segregated schools for African American children in the South, 1935–1969: A review of common themes and characteristics. *Review of Educational Research, 70*(3), 253–285.

Walker, V. S. (2001). African American teaching in the South: 1940–1960. *American Educational Research Journal, 38*(4), 751–779.

Walker, V. S. (2009). *Hello professor: A Black principal and professional leadership in the segregated South.* Chapel Hill: The University of North Carolina Press.

Walker, V. S. & Archung, K. N. (2003). The segregated schooling of Blacks in the Southern United States and South Africa. *Comparative Education Review, 47*, 21–40.

Walters, R. W. (2008). *The price of racial reconciliation.* Ann Arbor: The University of Michigan Press.

Watkins, W. H. (2001). *The White architects of Black education: Ideology and power in America, 1865–1954.* New York: Teachers College Press.

Watkins, W., Lewis, J., & Chou, V. (2001). *Race and education: The roles of history and society in educating African American students.* Boston: Allyn & Bacon.

Wells, A. S. (1993). *Time to choose: America at the crossroads of school choice policy.* New York: Hill and Wang.

Wells, A. S., Holmes, J. E., Revilla, A. T., & Atanda, A. K. (2009). *Both sides now: The story of school desegregation's graduates.* Berkeley: University of California Press.

Welner, K. G., & Oakes, J. (1996). (Li)Ability grouping: The new susceptibility of school tracking systems to legal challenges. *Harvard Educational Review, 66*(3), 451–471.

Woodson, C. G. (1933/1990). *The mis-education of the Negro.* Trenton, NJ: Africa World Press. (Original work published 1933)

Woodward, C. V. (1955). *The strange career of Jim Crow.* New York: Oxford University Press.

Yosso, T. J. (2005). Whose culture has capital? A critical race theory discussion of community cultural wealth. *Race Ethnicity and Education 8*(1), 69–91.

Yosso, T. J. (2006). *Critical race counterstories along the Chicana/Chicano educational pipeline.* New York: Routledge.

Zhao, Y. (2009). *Catching up or leading the way: American education in the age of globalization.* Alexandria, VA: ACSD.

Index

About the Author

Sonya Douglass Horsford is a senior resident scholar of education with the Lincy Institute at the University of Nevada, Las Vegas. Her research on educational leadership, policy, and politics in the post–Civil Rights era has appeared in journals such as *Educational Administration Quarterly*, *The Urban Review, Urban Education,* and *Journal of Negro Education.*